SHAKESPEARE
and the Energies of Drama

SHAKESPEARE
and the Energies
of Drama

MICHAEL GOLDMAN

PRINCETON UNIVERSITY PRESS
PRINCETON, NEW JERSEY
1972

Publication of this book has been aided by a
grant from the Whitney Darrow Publication Reserve
Fund of Princeton University Press

This book has been composed in Linotype Primer
Printed in the United States of America
by Princeton University Press

For Sarah Bergstein

Acknowledgments

A NUMBER of generous friends and colleagues—Eric Bentley, Erwin Glikes, Robert Hanning, Martin Meisel, Daniel Seltzer, and Edward Tayler—have helped me by reading my manuscript at crucial stages, offering careful criticism, putting themselves at my disposal, providing timely encouragement. I am very grateful to them, and in ways far too particular and extensive to do more than simply acknowledge here.

My wife, Eleanor, has been my closest critic. With sympathy, patience, and equally unfailing rigor, she has helped me discover my meaning a thousand times. Her intelligence has sustained, revived, emboldened me in every phase of this endeavor.

I am grateful to Professor E.D.H. Johnson and the Department of English of Princeton University for an invitation to lecture on a Shakespearean subject, which allowed me to test and develop a version of my sixth chapter. Most of my second chapter and portions of the third formed the basis of a talk given at Wesleyan University when I was a Visiting Fellow at the Center for the Humanities. My thanks go to the Center, its director, Professor Victor Gourevitch, and all those who participated in the lively and wide-ranging discussions that followed.

It may seem an impertinence to mention the name of G. E. Bentley here, as if to enlist his great authority on my behalf, and of course I intend nothing of the kind. But I am under obligation to him for the care and patient grace with which he attempted, years ago, to acquaint me with the methods and meaning of Shakespearean scholarship.

I would like also to mention with gratitude the name of John Northam, who provided much friendly and valuable insight into Shakespearean and other dramatic matters for the benefit of a young American at Cambridge.

The two men most immediately and deeply responsible for the thought that led me to this study have both died young. Alan Downer, who read an early draft and offered suggestions of the utmost importance, first introduced me to the serious study of the theater—with an intellectual hospitality as great as his knowledge, a sustained gesture of immense and genial comprehension that instructs and delights me still. Andrew Chiappe, who died before my work on the book had fairly begun, was my first and continuing teacher of Shakespeare and of poetry, a superb critic, ever a powerful example to me of imagination in the service of life. They were my guides, my colleagues, and my friends. It is not to be imagined that their worth or my indebtedness to them can be glanced at in this brief space or any space; but I wish to record here my pleasure in their memory, my sorrow in their loss, my great good luck in knowing them.

M. G.

New York
June 1971

Contents

SHAKESPEARE
and the Energies of Drama

I

Introduction: Shakespeare's Bodies

WHEN I talk about "meaning" in this book—as I often do—what I have in mind is the unique significance of our experience of a work of art. All experiences are unique, of course, just as all are to some extent interesting. Certain experiences, though, are of commanding interest—they awaken the mind to life, dominate memory, seem to enhance us to an extraordinary degree. It is natural and desirable to talk about such experiences and to try to say why and how they command us—what it is they do for and with our lives. In my view, this is what criticism should attempt for the experience of art, and the results it arrives at are what I call meaning.

Most of the experience I write about in these pages may be found only in the theater; my aims and methods spring from this fact. No single performance does justice to a great play, but plays exist in order to be made into performances. The experience of theatrical performance is so different from that of other arts that criticism must be very careful in approaching it. Drama confronts us with an unparalleled immediacy and inclusiveness. When we read a book many of the elements that engage our awareness while we read are irrelevant—the room in which we sit, the people around us, the light, our physical contact with the book itself, the wandering of our attention, even our momentary doubts as to what is happening on the page. In the theater, all such facts of the moment are pertinent, and our experience is entirely of the moment—moment after moment moving forward, gathering together and piling up physical and mental impressions. In writing about Shakespearean drama, I have tried to take into account the quality of the whole theatrical moment—our entire accumulating relation with what takes place on stage—and to seek a meaning for each play in the human significance of our response as an audience, in the life it awakens us to, the awarenesses it builds upon.

Inevitably, then, this is a study—though always in terms of particular examples—of the nature and meaning of dramatic experience itself. How are we engaged by drama? How do the components—words, acting, the disposition of figures on the stage, plot, and the rest—join in our minds as we sit in the theater? And what does the excitement and satisfaction with which we respond signify? Finally, what are useful tactics for talking about such matters? Can the shifting, evanescent, and multiple modes of response we experience in the theater be made the subject of exact and circumstantial criticism? The chapters that follow seek answers to these questions. But they also depend on certain assumptions about drama and the suitable ways of inquiring into it, and with these I had better begin.

I start out, as I have already suggested, with a notion of the crucially distinctive character of dramatic experience. Above all, there is its unique focus on the body. The play may rise in Shakespeare's imagination and come home to our own, but it takes place between two sets of bodies, ours and the actors'. An actor's profession and desire are to interest people with his body, and in the theater we are especially conscious of bodies, the actors' bodies, the bodies of the more or less closely packed audience (more closely packed in Shakespeare's theater than in ours), and whatever other images of the body are established or roused in our minds by what we see and hear. Our response to what the actor does with his body, to the strains that are put upon it and the graces it reveals, are very strong components of our response to the play as a whole.

I should emphasize that I am not trying to exalt the

actor at the expense of the text. In the theater there is no real separating of words and bodies. Shakespeare's text is primary, but the text implies an actor—a real person, not a puppet, not a reciter, not even an "interpreter." The personality and full bodily life of the actor are far more definitely present in his art than those of, say, the performers of music or ballet. These latter do not *enact* the works in which they appear; they are more nearly transmitters than actors. This is not to say that the pianist or dancer does not play a necessary or individual part in the experience of music or ballet, but to suggest their different relation to the work and to us. It is fair to say that musicians and dancers interpret the works in which they appear, and the verb is of course frequently applied to actors too; but in the latter case "interpret" should strike us as a little thin. "Mr. So-and-so will interpret the role of Antony tonight" sounds quaint, or as if the full power of the actor were not being invoked. The actor, we are aware, engages us in his presence as fully as he can. It is a created presence, to be sure, but created by him there and then, for us as part of an audience, an audience that comes to judge him and wonder at him and be delighted by him. We gossip more about actors' private lives than about other public figures' (and more about opera performers than pianists) because we have become involved with their bodies to a greater degree.

The audience is the other half of the dramatic equation, and its importance should not be overlooked. Throughout this book I have used the word "we" abundantly and unashamedly, not because I think I can speak for everyone's reactions, but because in the theater a play happens not to you or me but to us. It is our bodily presence, en masse, which completes the actor's being and sustains him in his quality, our heightened receptiveness as part of the peculiar community of silent strangers that constitutes an audience. We are intimately allied to our neighbors in the theater, respond-

5

ing not quite as individuals (the isolated laugh disrupts a comedy just as group laughter confirms it), and yet we are separated from them; once the play begins we no longer communicate with them freely, we do not behave (nor did Shakespeare's audience) like spectators at a sports event or political rally. We are more or less rapt, as if in the presence of a secret (in dreams, Freud tells us—in a remark that would seem to carry great relevance for the psychology of the theater—a group of strangers signifies a secret); part of the delight of the theater is that it recaptures the terror and pleasure of children spying on their elders. At the same time, though, the actor is like a child, performing as gracefully as he can to win the affection of the assembled grownups. Thus, our amusement and awe, pity and terror. And of course actors and audience are brothers, peers, adults, fully and humanly aware of each other—a relation which every Western dramatic convention modifies but must not destroy because its life as a convention depends upon it. The body of the actor works against the abstractness of his art; this is not a flaw in drama but its essence. All kinds of aesthetic distance may be established in the theater, but it will always manifest itself with a special tension because the interplay between live actor and bodily sensitive audience is constantly breaking the distance down.

We relate to each of the figures on stage, then, in a number of ways simultaneously. We relate to them as characters in a fiction, as real people moving and talking close to us, and as actors, who are at once both real and fictitious, and neither. Also we relate to them as parts of the entire stage activity, which likewise affects us bodily and directly. Ideally all these relations should be in our minds when we set out to examine a play; but there is also a need, at least at the present stage of critical understanding, to grow separately sensitive to the presence of each of the strands of feeling that run between actor and audience. In the chapters that follow

I have taken advantage of the distinctive qualities of a number of plays to emphasize now one, now another aspect of our response in the theater, though my aim in each is to throw light on the total experience. *Romeo and Juliet*, for example, allows me to raise the question of theatrical meaning in a rather direct and concentrated form. We are all familiar with the strong kinesthetic impression *Romeo and Juliet* usually makes in the theater. What can we say about the impression as a whole and its command over our minds? When the play has ended, certain details are likely to remain fixed in our memories as part of the cumulative experience: the lovers in characteristic poses, for example; crowds and gangs rushing across the stage with swords or torches; puns; outbursts of impatience; Juliet repeating Romeo's name. What is the unique meaning of an experience that fuses such impressions?

My method in discussing *Romeo and Juliet* is to begin with the theatrical sensation produced by the play as a whole. In the next chapter, I approach the question of meaning from the opposite direction, and consider a single character. Falstaff is such an attractive figure that he threatens to break up his play; his appeal is so physical that it takes on the disarming clarity of an idea. What is the precise nature of our relation to Falstaff as character and actor, and as a projection of our own bodily life?

Critically speaking, *Henry V* has lately proved more of a "problem play" than either *Romeo and Juliet* or *Henry IV*. Its obvious appeal to traditional patriotism and the equally obvious ironies of its treatment of patriotism have seemed difficult to reconcile in a way that does justice to all its elements and pleasures. In dealing with it I start with the manifest theatrical attractiveness of certain familiar passages and develop a view of the play as a whole by analyzing the relation they create between actors and audience.

One assumption that becomes prominent in the

discussion of *Henry V* is that the technical accomplishment of the actor will be an important part of our experience of the play and must be considered part of its design, even as the technical achievement of the lyric poet—rhyme scheme, patterns of sound, verbal resourcefulness—must be considered part of his poem's design. With acting, as with poetry, it is actually impossible to make a sharp distinction between "technique" and substance. Further, an actor may be expected to seek the maximum value that a scene allows him, and a good playwright should be expected to count on this. The theatrical weight of the wooing scene in *Henry V*, for example, must be calculated on the assumption that the actor playing the King will try to generate the most pleasure allowed him by the lines and the events of the scene. With *Hamlet* and *King Lear* I turn more comprehensively to the whole question of the actor as actor and the role as a chance to display powers which in themselves impress and delight an audience. Hamlet is a great acting part because (among other reasons) of the variety of actions he is called upon to perform, the quick changes he must make from one action to another. Lear is a great acting part because of what he must suffer, because of our sense that the actor who plays Lear must continually be outdoing himself in responding to pain. The contrast between the two kinds of acting achievement and our responses to them does much to characterize the two plays.

Another very important means of controlling our response in the theater is the orchestration of stage movement. From his earliest works, Shakespeare handles motifs of movement with the same richness of suggestion and recurrence that distinguishes his verbal imagery. A number of chapters, notably those on *Romeo and Juliet* and *Hamlet*, treat these effects in passing. My seventh chapter, however, takes as its central concern a particular piece of recurrent choreographic design in *Coriolanus* and considers how it affects our feeling for the hero and his situation. (Strikingly, the pattern of crowd movement discussed has perhaps its profoundest effect in a scene where crowds do not appear.)

No audience, finally, ever forgets it is at a play, and this self-consciousness contributes to the drama, too. It may make itself felt simply as expectation, a sense of the possible or permissible shapes the play may take. When Hamlet breaks in upon Claudius at prayer, part of our reaction to the scene depends on our confidence that the play is barely half over and that an "accidental" revenge is not what its machinery has been preparing us for. Part of our pleasure in Falstaff has to do with our knowledge that he has eventually to be removed from the stage in order for the necessary business of the play to continue. Here our expectation as to the shape and nature of the action unfolding before us enters into our local response.

In the chapters on *Hamlet* and *Lear* I have occasion to note another use of our self-consciousness. This comes at moments when our relation to the play involves an awareness of the special character of what is being done to us as an audience. Let me oversimplify a little for the present. We have to ask at moments in *Lear*, "Why so much torture?"; in *Hamlet*, "Why so much left in doubt?" At these points we are made aware—though perhaps not at a fully conscious level—of our theatrical appetites, of some of the desires we go to a play to satisfy. In the last plays, our appetite for a whole complex of dramatic satisfactions, particularly the happy ending, is played upon to such a degree that it becomes practically part of the story. The theme of "art" in *The Tempest* and *The Winter's Tale* is clearly understood, for example, only if it is seen as developed in the playhouse against the audience's sharpened sense of its relation, as audience, to the art of the theater. And it is in this self-conscious theatrical con-

CHAPTER I

text that many of the plays' other themes fuse and have their life. The last plays may in fact be seen as Shakespeare's own exploration of the meaning of dramatic experience, and my concluding pages try to suggest what, in its broadest sense, I take this meaning to be. It should by now be clear that when I say "body" I do not mean something distinct from mind. Our heightened bodily awareness in the theater includes all our modes of consciousness. It is an awareness of the self in its fullest presence—multiple, quickening, transient, solid, passionate, imagining, desiring. Indeed it is this special awareness of self that gives the theater its unique capacity—felt by audience and actors alike—to be both self-liberating and self-confronting. Discovery of the self and release of the self are not only common themes of the drama; they are what happens in the theater as the drama unfolds.

This is what lies behind my choice of Shakespeare's non-dramatic verse as a point of departure. It is only reasonable to relate everything we know about Shakespeare to his dramatic achievement. The impulse toward drama in an artist, like the impulse toward poetry, involves the whole disposition of the being. Shakespeare is not a poet with a knack for "dramatizing" his conceptions, any more than Dante is a Christian with a knack for poetizing his philosophy. Shakespeare's non-dramatic poetry reflects his dramatic bent as anything about his life might be expected to—not because it shows us a gift for action or dialogue (it doesn't especially), but because it shows us a response to life for which drama was finally necessary.

Accordingly, I begin with a chapter on *Venus and Adonis, Lucrece,* and the sonnets. In them may be discerned a bent for certain situations and arrangements of material which draw attention to what Shakespeare calls the "unsounded self," a condition of being that can be fully explored only in drama. What is involved is the sense of a self or selves within the self, of powers, feelings, and styles that come to fruition only through the stress of encounter. This implies a conception of human possibility, and indeed of human necessity, requiring drama for its articulation and satisfaction. As such it provides a basis for dramatic development that may be found in all the plays considered in this volume. The connection between this "pre-dramatic" material and the critical method I have been discussing is not at all adventitious. For I hope to make clear that it is exactly in this—the necessary relation between the fully "sounded" self and the special kinds of awareness that an audience has in the theater—that the meaning of dramatic experience ultimately resides.

II

The Unsounded Self

MY STUDENTS have a quick, one might say instinctive, response to *Venus and Adonis*. The poem is queer, they insist. And like the intelligent young men they are, they make a good case for it. Isn't there a "reversal of roles" throughout? Look at how feminine Adonis is—and narcissistic. He likes hunting with his friends, and, they say—several raising their hands, pursuing the question in chorus—you know what that means.

And Venus! Not only is she the "aggressor," who attacks Adonis like a starving eagle, but there are clear analogies drawn between her and the wild boar that kills him. She imagines Adonis down and trapped by the boar at the same time as she is holding him down and trapped in her arms. Like Venus, the boar tries to "kiss" Adonis and goes for his groin. The long tusk penetrates his "soft flank," blood flows, there is weeping. It is a "symbolic rape." At the end, Venus plucks the flower into which he has been transformed:

She crops the stalk, and in the breach appears
Green-dropping sap, which she compares to tears.[1]
(1175-76)

She has completed the process by violating him anew.

The important point is that my students are not entirely wrong. As a teacher I have to be pleased with a response so intense and circumstantial. They have taken the crucial first step and opened themselves to the poem. What they fail to recognize is that they have

[1] Citations from Shakespeare's works follow the New Cambridge Edition, ed. W. A. Neilson and C. J. Hill (Cambridge, Mass., 1942).

opened themselves rather more than they have opened *Venus and Adonis*. The two processes are related; more than they are likely to be aware, they are implicated in the poem. They are upset by what they consider to be Venus's masculine thrust. It does not conform to "mature sexual experience" as they imagine it to be. They still believe that as grown men they will wield the thrust, take pleasure, and remain unmoved—moving others they will be themselves as stone—but this is adolescent fantasy, the fantasy indeed of the hunt, which engages them even in the classroom. Though they may actually fulfill it, now or later, in their own sexual encounters, it will be only as a result of Adonis-like cloture and not from adult openness to the unsettling onslaughts of Venus, which bear the imagery of time and death. They are still much closer to Adonis than they guess, standing as they do at the healthy peak of youthful narcissism.

Adonis's kind of beautiful adolescence—narcissistic, self-sufficient, charming, and protected, with a beauty that clearly has not encountered the full stresses of an adult world—is rather like certain kinds of high "literary" style in poetry, and such closed stylistic elegance is present in *Venus and Adonis*. But there is another stylistic strain, a cruder realism, a robust humor that comes not from words, as the Ovidian wit of the poem does, but from things. Critics have usually associated the more realistic voice with Shakespeare's "Stratford youth" or some such, and seen it as unpolished, a bumpkinish streak not fully accommodated to the elegant mode Shakespeare was trying to master. It is hard to understand how an idea so removed from normal experience, either of life or poetry, can have attained currency. First, verbal polish—mastery of an accepted form of wit—is the easiest thing for any gifted young man on the make to achieve, especially if his gift is literary (or histrionic). As a piece of witty Ovidian titillation the poem not only passed muster with the young blades of Shakespeare's day, but proved a great and lasting success. And even if these contemporary readers, immersed in Elizabethan gallantry and brought up on Ovid, were somehow not so susceptible to patches of provincial clumsiness as our own literary experts, is it likely that Shakespeare, even at twenty-eight, was not aware that the style of

> Full gently now she takes him by the hand,
> A lily prison'd in a gaol of snow,
> Or ivory in an alabaster band;
> So white a friend engirts so white a foe.
> This beauteous combat, wilful and unwilling,
> Show'd like two silver doves that sit a-billing.
> (361-66)

was different from

> Round-hoof'd, short-jointed, fetlocks shag
> and long,
> Broad breast, full eye, small head, and nostril
> wide,
> High crest, short ears, straight legs and pass-
> ing strong,
> Thin mane, thick tail, broad buttock, tender
> hide:
> Look, what a horse should have he did not
> lack,
> Save a proud rider on so proud a back.
> (295-300)

It must be assumed he found the mixture of the two acceptable.

The presence of two styles gives the poem its real impact and reflects its story. The confrontation of a lovely, if immature self-sufficiency with the more demanding and cruder energies of life that both Venus and the enraged boar force upon Adonis is clearly echoed by the interplay between the witty, conventional, erotic elegance of the poem and its colloquial verve, realism, and frequent comic gusto. The encounter between Venus and Adonis may be thought of as a lily prisoned in a gaol of snow, something *raffiné*, a witty juxtaposition of surfaces, but the poem also makes us see it as Venus wants Adonis to feel it—as something like the power-laden coupling of animals. The rougher style jostles and shakes up the more conceited one as the goddess of love shakes up the young man. The confrontation is dramatic and, as I shall suggest, characteristically Shakespearean.

The artful blending of the two styles is largely responsible for the distinctive charm and liveliness of the poem. In the very first stanza we feel a certain hearty abruptness in the couplet introducing Venus that comes in on the heels of the mythological, witty, titillating conceit of the quatrain:

> Even as the sun with purple-colour'd face
> Had ta'en his last leave of the weeping morn,
> Rose-cheek'd Adonis hied him to the chase;
> Hunting he lov'd, but love he laugh'd to
>   scorn.
> Sick-thoughted Venus makes amain unto
>   him,
> And like a bold-fac'd suitor gins to woo him.

The slight, jostling interplay—one style jiggling the other's elbow—is also achieved at various moments by introducing a colloquial or roughening phrase into passages of conventional delicacy or rhetoric:

> For, by this black-fac'd Night, Desire's foul
>   nurse,
> Your treatise makes me like you worse and
>   worse.   (773-74)

> These blue-vein'd violets whereon we lean
> Never can blab, nor know not what we mean.
>   (125-26)

15

The second example suggests another similar effect the poem obtains by combining precise, minute realism with hypersensitive, even precious observation:

> Or, as the snail, whose tender horns being
> hit,
> Shrinks backward in his shelly cave with
> pain,
> . . . So, at his bloody view, her eyes are fled
> Into the deep-dark cabins of her head . . .
> (1033-38)

or in the famous comparison of Adonis to a "dive-dapper peering through a wave" (85-87). Other devices might be distinguished. To criticize the poem for its vagaries of expression, for being "unintentionally comic," is to miss the point. Venus's wooing of Adonis is as slapstick as it is sensual, but the combination makes the poem effective:

> Over one arm the lusty courser's rein,
> Under her other was the tender boy,
> Who blush'd and pouted in a dull disdain,
> With leaden appetite, unapt to toy;
> She red and hot as coals of glowing fire,
> He red for shame, but frosty in desire.
> (31-36)

In the passage just quoted, Adonis's rose-cheeked innocence is contrasted to Venus's more passionate complexion, just as in the first stanza his face is contrasted with the sun's. Later, after his encounter with the boar, his "purple" blood gives its color to the flower Venus will carry in her bosom:

> By this, the boy that by her side lay kill'd
> Was melted like a vapour from her sight,
> And in his blood that on the ground lay
> spill'd,
> A purple flower sprung up, check'red with
> white,

> Resembling well his pale cheeks and the
>   blood
> Which in round drops upon their whiteness
>   stood.   (1165-70)

"Purple" to the Elizabethans was a shade of red, but
it is clear from the first stanza that it is a more intense
shade than, for example, rose. At the poem's end, red
and white are still Adonis's colors, but no longer the
conventional poetic formula for the innocent elegance
of rosy cheeks and creamy skin. They are instead the
red and white of blood and murdered flesh. He is closer
to Venus now, in intensity and experience.

Like many very young men, Adonis seems to want
the fruits of experience before he risks the difficulties.
He wants, as we say, to find himself:

> "Fair queen," quoth he, "if any love you owe
>   me,
> Measure my strangeness with my unripe
>   years;
> Before I know myself, seek not to know me."
>   (523-25)

Adonis is an early instance of a familiar Shakespearean
type—the closed-off or cautious man who is not ready
to hazard enough of himself for the woman who loves
him.

Charm, self-sufficiency, the mastery of a conventional style are all attributes of the successful young
man. And they may seem threatened by the deeper
reaches of experience. It might be interesting to spec-
ulate to what extent Shakespeare had his own situation in mind. Certainly he returns to versions of this
conflict with great frequency. More valuably, however,
it may be observed how essentially dramatic the theme
is. The powers and problems of this kind of self can
only be released by forced encounter, and it is exactly
this that forms the basis of much of Shakespeare's

early drama. *The Comedy of Errors*, for example, presents a young man, Antipholus of Syracuse, who seems to hold back from the relationships offered by the world about him, a young man who is also engaged in a hunt (for his other self, his twin) and who becomes the hunted. The action of the play thrusts him, unwilling and bewildered, into a complicated web of relationships; in the course of it he finds a wife. The pattern is developed much more fully and finds a more characteristic form in *Love's Labour's Lost, Romeo and Juliet,* and *Much Ado About Nothing,* and even in *Two Gentlemen of Verona, The Taming of the Shrew,* and *The Merchant of Venice.* We are introduced to charming young men, masters of some kind of high style, usually verbal, who hold back in various ways from a full engagement of the self, often from full sexual engagement (the scholars' pact in *Love's Labour's Lost,* Benedick's insistence on bachelorhood). Not surprisingly, they show an Adonis-like tendency to hunt in groups, banding together for study, travel, adventure, and romance. The action tests them. They usually start out in a world of attractive artifice or sport and are threatened or changed by situations that are in some way "realer" and more serious. Certain motifs seem grouped together: at one pole education, sport, male friendship, the language of elegant literary or dramatic convention; at the other, love that leads to marriage and a language or activity that at least by contrast suggests reality (Shylock's bargain, which he calls "a merry sport"; Beatrice's "Kill Claudio!"). In most of the plays contrasting styles appear that heighten our sense of the real as opposed to the artificial, the adult as opposed to the adolescent (Petruchio as opposed to the other wooers, Juliet as compared to Rosaline, the challenges to Berowne's rhetorical style and his own efforts to alter it).

In these plays, we get an exploitation and working-out of an idea that is at best implicit in *Venus and*

Adonis: that the adult, engaged, open self (or selves) lies *within* the unchallenged self and is only revealed in action. This is the theme of the "unsounded self," surely the great motif in early Shakespeare. The phrase comes from the closing lines of *Lucrece*, when the focus suddenly shifts to Junius Brutus, who reveals an authority he has hitherto disguised:

> But now he throws that shallow habit by
> Wherein deep policy did him disguise;
> And arm'd his long-hid wits advisedly
> To check the tears in Collatinus' eyes.
> "Thou wronged lord of Rome," quoth he,
>   "arise.
> Let my unsounded self, suppos'd a fool,
> Now set thy long-experienc'd wit to school."
>   (1814-20)

The notion of unsounded selves, of components of character that may be revealed under the stress of action, is not only of interest from the point of view of Shakespeare's development as a dramatist, but is of great importance to the poem. Once its presence is recognized, many of the work's obscurities become clear—which is to say they reveal at least an organizing intention behind passages that otherwise have seemed unnecessary or diffuse. The lengthy description of the painting of Troy, for example, is generally considered to be an egregious digression, no more than a "means to mourn some newer way" as the poem calls it (1365). That *Lucrece* is long for modern tastes there can be no doubt, but the painting stanzas are among its most attractive. With almost any other work of Shakespeare we would expect that what attracts reveals, and this turns out to be equally true of *Lucrece*.

The description of the painting is marked by its emphasis on crowds of people. But what we are directed to notice and respond to in the crowds is their populousness, the number of individual members they contain. The passage opens with a quick survey of numerous figures, none seen very clearly, some only partially, with equal weight given to laborers, cowards, and commanders:

> There might you see the labouring pioner
> Begrim'd with sweat, and smeared all with
>   dust;
> And from the towers of Troy there would
>   appear
> The very eyes of men through loop-holes
>   thrust,
> Gazing upon the Greeks with little lust.
> Such sweet observance in this work was had,
> That one might see those far-off eyes look
>   sad.
>
> In great commanders grace and majesty
> You might behold, triumphing in their faces;
> In youth, quick bearing and dexterity;
> And here and there the painter interlaces
> Pale cowards, marching on with trembling
>   paces;
> Which heartless peasants did so well resemble,
> That one would swear he saw them quake
>   and tremble.   (1380-93)

The description of Nestor occupies one stanza, while three are devoted to the crowd thronging round him. Here, too, the trick of singling out separate parts of the body as composing the crowd is continued:

> Here one man's hand lean'd on another's
>   head,
> His nose being shadowed by his neighbour's
>   ear.   (1415-16)

Even Achilles is seen only as hidden in the throng:

20

. . . for Achilles' image stood his spear,
Gripp'd in an armed hand; himself, behind,
Was left unseen, save to the eye of mind.
A hand, a foot, a face, a leg, a head,
Stood for the whole to be imagined.

(1424-28)

There are of course many reasons for keeping
crowds before an audience, and Shakespeare will use
them in plays on Roman themes later in his career.
But in *Julius Caesar* and *Coriolanus* the emphasis will
be on the crowds as massive unities. Here the emphasis is on the numberless individuals and parts of individuals they contain. I would suggest that the effect
is to reinforce the sense of multiple selves within the
self, that can be released or experienced at times of
stress, at moments of conflict, violence, or grief like
the taking of Troy or the rape of Lucrece. It is significant that, viewing the painting, Lucrece identifies most
of all not with any single figure but with Troy itself—
with the entire thronged scene.

Attention is drawn to throngs elsewhere in the poem.
After the rape, Tarquin's soul is seen as the princess
of a temple:

To whose weak ruins muster troops of cares,
To ask the spotted princess how she fares.

(720-21)

When Lucrece sits down to write to Collatine, a great
number of thoughts and emotions crowd her mind:

Much like a press of people at a door,
Throng her inventions, which shall go before.

(1301-02)

Earlier her breath has come "thronging" (1041)
through her lips. And later, when she has killed herself,
her body lying in its blood will be compared to a

21

late-sack'd island . . .
Bare and unpeopled in this fearful flood.
(1740-41)

In all cases the figure of the crowd is used to suggest some sort of varied population inside the body, a throng of multiple possibilities or competing selves.

Clearly we are able to respond the more easily to this series of associations because Tarquin's act is treated at great length as an example of deceitful appearance or a surprising revelation of what may lie within the self. Contemplating the painting of Troy, Lucrece is particularly troubled by the attractive portrait of Sinon. "Some shape in Sinon's was abus'd" (1529), she decides at first, meaning that the body and face represented as Sinon's must actually be someone else's because it is so fair. But then she recalls Tarquin's perfidy. The comparison is of course a commonplace. It is not surprising that Tarquin or Sinon should be charged with having an unexpected self inside. But the presence of this major and obvious motif helps invest the repeated images of crowds with suggestive force and vice versa.

At the end of the poem the heroine is associated even more strongly with the idea of multiple selves. The emergence of Brutus as a political figure immediately follows a curious debate between Lucretius and Collatine. Each claims that Lucrece belonged to him, and they compete with cries of " 'my laughter!' and 'My wife!' " It is at this point that Brutus

Seeing such emulation in their woe,
Began to clothe his wit in state and pride.
(1808-09)

Brutus's response, proposing the expulsion of the Tarquins and triggering civil rebellion, shows that Lucrece is also an example of an unsounded self. The heroine who now emerges is not the betrayed woman of the long soliloquies, not the wife or daughter that husband and father claim her to be, but Lucrece, the political rallying cry.

The self propelled to the surface by events may be a surprising, even unsettling one. The conclusion of the poem connects interestingly with Lucrece's earlier denunciation of Helen in the painting scene:

> Show me the strumpet that began this stir,
> That with my nails her beauty I may tear.
>
> (1471-72)

The comment itself has an odd resonance because Helen, as the poem has recently stressed, is also a raped woman. Lucrece does not identify with her, of course, but with the entire crowded city of Troy that Sinon betrayed:

> As Priam him did cherish,
> So did I Tarquin; so my Troy did perish.
>
> (1546-47)

She is chiefly angry with Helen because her rape became the occasion for Troy's destruction:

> Why should the private pleasure of some one
> Become the public plague of many moe?
> Let sin, alone committed, light alone
> Upon his head that hath transgressed so;
> Let guiltless souls be freed from guilty woe:
> For one's offence why should so many fall,
> To plague a private sin in general?
>
> (1478-84)

But at the poem's end Lucrece's private act will likewise become the occasion for public events of world-altering proportions.

If Lucrece, Tarquin, and Brutus are compared to the victims, villains, and political heroes of *Titus Andronicus*, the relation of the theme of the unsounded self to Shakespeare's developing sense of tragic action

23

becomes clear. Lucius, at the end of *Titus*, is simply the good son restoring just rule. Brutus, though certainly recognizable as the great liberator of tradition, is also the canny opportunist seizing an unexpected event to make a carefully plotted political move. In *Lucrece*, there is concern with inner debate, choice, self-reproach, relatively complex motivation, unexpected revelations of character. This is not to claim for the poem an appeal it does not have; Tarquin and Lucrece are still not very interesting as individuals. The point, however, is not that their actions surprise or disturb us, but that they are surprising and disturbing to themselves. The full powers of the self emerge only in encounter, and they are complicating, even threatening in their multiplicity.

Shakespeare's concern with the discovery of the unsounded self seems to be reflected even in the syntax of his poems. At least, it appears to account for a peculiar construction that lends bite and drive to passages in *Venus and Adonis*, *Lucrece*, and the sonnets:

> Narcissus so himself himself forsook . . .
> (*Venus*, 161)
> So in thyself thyself art made away . . . (763)

> And for himself himself he must forsake
> (*Lucrece*, 157)
> When he himself himself confounds, betrays
> (160)
> Himself himself seek every hour to kill (998)
> Myself, thy friend, will kill myself, thy foe
> (1196)

> Thyself thy foe, to thy sweet self too cruel
> (Sonnet 1)
> then you were
> Yourself again after yourself's decease
> (Sonnet 13)

In the history of the English language, Shakespeare presides over the change of the word "self" from a purely grammatical indicator to something like the complex term it is today.[2] The "himself himself" figure looks forward to the self-baffled heroes of the middle tragedies ("Brutus with himself at war") and helps impart a sense of a closed self within the individual and at the same time of some inner energy or second self working to split it open.

An Adonis-like young man is at the center of most of the sonnets, and it has been recognized that they too, in Edward Hubler's phrase, probe "the economy of the closed heart."[3] But their concern is not primarily with observing this self or recording the poet's infatuation. Once again, the problem of "sounding" is paramount.

Of the selves recognizable beneath the glazed exterior of the young man, the crucial one for Shakespeare is what he calls the "sweet self":

> For, having traffic with thyself alone,
> Thou of thyself thy sweet self dost deceive.
>
>   (4, 9-10)

The sweet self is both the source of charm in this closed and self-sufficient personality and also the reason why the young man's self deserves and needs to be opened.

[2] Shakespeare never fully invests the word with its peculiar modern meanings, nor of course is he the first to seem aware of notions we might use "self" to describe. But the thought and the word are working to join each other in Shakespeare as in none of his contemporaries. Something of this may conveniently be seen from a comparison of the entries under "self" in a Spenser concordance and their contexts with those in a Shakespeare concordance, and of the uses of "self," "himself," "thyself," etc. in the *Amoretti* and Sidney's *Astrophel and Stella*, say, with those in the sonnets. The *OED* entry under "self" is very revealing too, but needs to be studied carefully. See Appendix A.

[3] *The Sense of Shakespeare's Sonnets* (Princeton, 1952), pp. 95-109.

It was for his sweetness that the Shakespeare of *Venus and Adonis* and the sonnets was fashionably famed. He was "sweet Mr. Shakespeare," or as Meres wrote: "The sweet wittie soule of *Ouid* liues in mellifluous & hony-tongued *Shakespeare*, witnes his *Venus and Adonis*, his *Lucrece*, his sugred Sonnets among his priuate friends, &c."[4] The sweet self, however, is the inner and valuable counterpart of the sweet appearance, and its importance is reflected in the sonnets' emphasis upon inner and outer (perfume and flower, substance and show, truth and beauty, etc.). The sweet self is attractive, closed-off, in part attractive because closed-off, but also threatened by being closed off. The sweet self can only be realized by being released. It may release and even preserve itself in action—by having children, for example, or by being "kind" to friends. This is one way it may be sounded; it may also be sounded in art.

For, finally, it is the sounding of the young man's self in poetry that becomes the central activity of the first 126 sonnets—more important than either the young man himself or his conduct toward the poet. Very early in the sequence, the theme of artistic immortality replaces the injunction to reproduce. It is the poet's relation to the friend that is the subject of the sonnets, and his friendship—the complex state of mind he develops toward his friend's sweet self—is not very different in its processes from his activity as an artist. The sonnets, it is true, sometimes say simply, "This young man is wonderful," but more often they say, "Look how wonderful he remains in spite of all vicissitudes, in my mind and in my poetry." Fair, kind, and true is the poet's theme, and he makes it work even though we *know* that the young man is neither kind nor true and cannot be fair forever. The sonnets celebrate their own achievement.

[4] E. K. Chambers, *William Shakespeare* (Oxford, 1930), II, 194.

The familiar eighteenth sonnet may serve as an example. Its beginning leads the reader to expect only the simplest kind of structure, the plainest loving hyperbole:

> Shall I compare thee to a summer's day?
> Thou art more lovely and more temperate:

And as the poem proceeds, the comparison seems to be working itself out in the predictable way:

> Rough winds do shake the darling buds of
>   May,
> And summer's lease hath all too short a date;
> Sometime too hot the eye of heaven shines,
> And often is his gold complexion dimm'd;
> And every fair from fair sometime declines,
> By chance or nature's changing course un-
>   trimm'd:
> But thy eternal summer shall not fade . . .

But it suddenly becomes clear that the terms of the comparison have shifted. The poem is no longer about the differences between the young man and a summer's day but between a summer's day and poetry about him:

> But thy eternal summer shall not fade
> Nor lose possession of that fair thou ow'st;
> Nor shall Death brag thou wand'rest in his
>   shade,
> When in eternal lines to time thou grow'st;
> So long as men can breathe or eyes can see,
> So long lives this, and this gives life to thee.

The young man may indeed be lovelier and more temperate than a summer's day, but he too is subject to mutability and imperfection. Like every fair from fair he sometimes declines, which in the light of the other sonnets is putting it mildly. Thus, the opening line turns out to have asked not so much, "In what way are you more beautiful than a summer's day?" as "What will happen—what will be the value of the result—if I write a poem comparing you to a summer's day?" or more plainly, taking into account the poem's conclusion, "In what way is poetry about you more beautiful than you are?"

By virtue of the poet's devotion, even the friend's sin becomes part of the artistic process, which involves not only the creation of poems but the creation of the poet's self. A sweet self is released for us in the sonnets, but it is at least as much the poet's as the friend's. It is *my* love, Shakespeare writes in 61 that presents you to me:

> O, no! thy love, though much, is not so great;
> It is my love that keeps mine eye awake;
> Mine own true love that doth my rest defeat.
>
> (9-11)

There is a double meaning in "mine own true love," and it is very important to the sonnets.

In the next sonnet the poet turns to praising his own beauty. I am deep in self-love, he says, because my friend is now "myself." His own self is sweetened and preserved, apparently by the friend's. But the sonnet must be read in context. Just as the preceding sonnet has reminded us that the friend is vividly present to Shakespeare's imagination not by virtue of his own wavering affections, but through the poet's true love, so 63 emphasizes that, like the poet in 62, the friend too will be destroyed by time. Again like the poet, he will be preserved—by poetry.

The sweetness of the friend's self, though it may be called into question (or even "turn sour") by his acts, remains safe as a kind of artifact in the poet's possession. The friend's self may even be said to create a sweet self in the poet, and this is the point of 62:

Sin of self-love possesseth all mine eye
And all my soul and all my every part;
And for this sin there is no remedy,
It is so grounded inward in my heart.
Methinks no face so gracious is as mine,
No shape so true, no truth of such account;
And for myself mine own worth do define,
As I all other in all worth surmount.
But when my glass shows me myself indeed,
Beated and chopp'd with tann'd antiquity,
Mine own self-love quite contrary I read;
Self so self-loving were iniquity.
'Tis thee, myself, that for myself I praise,
Painting my age with beauty of thy days.

Here Shakespeare adopts, it would seem, the narcissism we readily associate with his friend, though we
are aware that the poet's character is actually quite
different—loyal, loving, and open to love, "kind and
true." It is ironically appropriate, though, because the
self he loves is his friend's self in him. But as the other
sonnets show, the friend's self that he cherishes is kind
and true, too. The poet has created an immortal open
self out of his friend's closed unsounded one—a development that recalls the apotheosis of Adonis—and he
has sounded his own self in the process.

The paradox is essential to the sonnets. The marriage of true minds is what the first 126 sonnets
achieve—not what they record. Fairness, kindness, and
truth are created out of wavering and defective material, and the contrast heightens the value of what has
been accomplished. The value, in fact, resides in the
contrast. The fixed star's worth depends on the existence of wandering barks; what time takes away poetry
engrafts anew. The great force of Time is of course
always part of the sonnets' universe, and the sequence
just discussed issues, in 64, in one of the great expressions of devouring Time's vast corrosive power:

When I have seen by Time's fell hand defaced
The rich proud cost of outworn buried age;
When sometime lofty towers I see down-
    rased,
And brass eternal slave to mortal rage;
When I have seen the hungry ocean gain
Advantage on the kingdom of the shore,
And the firm soil win of the wat'ry main,
Increasing store with loss and loss with store;
When I have seen such interchange of state,
Or state itself confounded to decay;
Ruin hath taught me thus to ruminate,
That Time will come and take my love away.
This thought is as a death, which cannot
    choose
But weep to have that which it fears to lose.

"Store" and "loss" are opposed in the vocabulary
of the sonnets, but are actually present—here and elsewhere—as part of a single process. The paradox is that
store can be gained with loss and loss with store. There
is a store that poetry or love can make out of the continuing experience of loss, of physical and moral decay,
of the dangerous opening of the self to the world. We
are left with a sense that "store" finally in some way
depends upon the phenomenon of loss, cannot be
achieved without it. The apparently self-sufficient store
of those who husband nature's riches from expense is,
on the other hand, especially vulnerable to loss. It is
time and the endless process of loss that makes life
inevitably dramatic, and in the face of time all lasting
value can be realized—the sweet self released—only
through encounter.

The Dark Lady sonnets take their place in the sequence as Venus takes her place next to Adonis—with
the force of dramatic confrontation. I have in mind
not so much the confrontation of the lady with the
other characters as the confrontation of the sonnets

about her with all the preceding sonnets. One of the reasons why we are so lured to biographical conjecture by these concluding sonnets, why the Dark Lady and the trouble she creates seem so real, is that the structure and method of the sonnets encourage us to see her as realer, in the sense of more difficult and less coped with by poetic expression, than anything in the earlier sonnets. The process of poetic creation is referred to only once in this section (130), and there poetry is mocked by contrast with the reality of the lady whose eyes are nothing like the sun. The distinction between eye and heart maintained in the earlier sonnets breaks down. The heart is no longer seduced by the eye but both are seduced for an undiscoverable reason:

> Why should my heart think that a several plot
> Which my heart knows the wide world's com-
> > mon place?
> Or mine eyes seeing this, say this is not,
> To put fair truth upon so foul a face?
> > (137, 9-12)

In the case of the Dark Lady, there is no appearance of beauty to begin with as there was with the friend; there is not even an illusory sweet self to store. The equation of loss and store is unbalanced except in the brittle poise of the mutually deceiving sonnets:

> Therefore I lie with her and she with me,
> And in our faults by lies we flattered be.
> > (138, 13-14)

Once more the dramatic pattern inherent to the idea of the unsounded self emerges. In the first 126 sonnets Shakespeare has set up a system, a vindication of love and poetry that is as self-sufficient and self-contained in its way as Adonis, only to expose it to a tougher, more sensual and threatening realism. Like *Venus and Adonis* and *Lucrece*, the sonnets are neither dramatic nor undramatic but pre-dramatic. They imply drama because the theme of the unsounded self implies drama. The drama of the sonnets, like that of the narrative poems, lies not in the exploitation of scenes or dramatic voices, but in the exposure of the closed self to urgent and dangerous possibilities.

The sounding of the self is a development rather like the one that usually takes place in the career of a good poet—from self-delight, free of the world, to delight by encounter with the world. There is risk in the encounter, just as there is pleasure, charm, and even power in holding back. We know nothing about Shakespeare from the ages of twenty to twenty-eight, except that he seems to have left his family and become an actor, that he must have been very gifted, and that when he does emerge he emerges rapidly. The pleasures of holding back as well as the need to risk deeper soundings must have been at least as vivid to him as they are to the ordinary man—or as they are, for example, to Hamlet. "I have that within which passeth show," announces "I have a self which cannot be sounded by drama." It is both a holding back and a challenge. It is suggestive that Hamlet seems to be about eighteen at his play's beginning but turns out to be thirty at its end.

III

Romeo and Juliet

The Meaning of a Theatrical Experience

EVERYTHING in *Romeo and Juliet* is intense, impatient, threatening, explosive. We are caught up in speed, heat, desire, riots, running, jumping, rapid-fire puns, dirty jokes, extravagance, compressed and urgent passion, the pressure of secrets, fire, blood, death. Visually, the play remains memorable for a number of repeated images—street brawls, swords flashing to the hand, torches rushing on and off, crowds rapidly gathering. The upper stage is used frequently, with many opportunities for leaping or scrambling or stretching up and down and much play between upper and lower areas. The dominant bodily feelings we get as an audience are oppressive heat, sexual desire, a frequent whiz-bang exhilarating kinesthesia of speed and clash, and above all a feeling of the keeping-down and separation of highly charged bodies, whose pressure toward release and whose sudden discharge determine the rhythm of the play.

The thematic appropriateness of these sensations to Shakespeare's first great tragedy of the unsounded self is obvious enough, perhaps too obvious. Shakespeare's tragic heroes usually pass from isolation to isolation. Romeo cannot be one of the boys or Hamlet one of his northern world's competent, adaptable young men. At the beginning the isolation is that of the unsounded self, some form of self-sufficiency, remoteness, or withdrawal. The hero strikes us as a kind of closed structure. He very clearly carries a packaged energy; on first meeting him we recognize the container and the seal. (Think of Romeo or Hamlet for swift opening indications of these.) The ultimate isolation comes in the rupture of the package, the energy's discharge. The drama marks the change. Romeo and Juliet are isolated by the sudden demands of love returned, and the world of their play reflects the violence of the transformation.

The type of outline just given is useful but treacherous. It is useful because it sharpens our sense of the Shakespearean dramatic situation and gives us a reasonably pertinent norm by which to measure individual developments. But to follow it out in detail, to translate each tragedy back into the outline, to tell it like a story for any of the plays would be to lose exactly what makes the idea of the unsounded self important—that it is basic to drama, something far different from story or subject or theme. This is what is wrong with thinking about theatrical impressions in terms of thematic appropriateness, as a kind of varnish over the poetry and plot.

What ideally has to be done and is perhaps more easily attempted for *Romeo and Juliet* than for later plays is to talk about what the experience of the whole amounts to. The impression is strong and distinctive; why do we mark it as we do? The problem is to take all the elements that affect us in the theater and examine them as they arrange themselves in our response, asking what relevance this configuration bears to our lives.

If we try to see what the deep effect of the combination of these elements is, the crucial question is that of the relation that connects the plot, the visual spectacle, and the wordplay. Clearly they share a common busyness, suddenness, and violence. "These violent delights have violent ends" is enough to explain their congruence at least superficially. But it does not account for the richness of our response to the elaborate detail of the drama. Nor does it account for the peculiar aptness we sense in certain kinds of detail. Why are there so many puns and such obscene ones? Why should Mercutio and the Nurse be given long, digressive bravura speeches? Why is the balcony stressed, and the athleticism it entails? Why should certain lines like "Wherefore art thou Romeo?" or "What's in a name?" or "A feasting presence full of light" stick in the memory? The last may be explained by its "beauty out of context" —always a doubtful procedure—but the other lines resist even that easy question-begging method, and consequently give us a good place to begin.

"Wherefore art thou Romeo?"

Romeo's name presents a problem to others besides Juliet but she characteristically sees more deeply into the difficulty. For it is not enough to decide whether Romeo should be called humors, madman, passion, lunatic, villain, coward, boy, Capulet, Montague, or even Romeo. The question is really why he must have a name at all. *Romeo and Juliet* is a tragedy of naming, a tragedy in which at times Romeo's name seems to be the villain:

> As if that name,
> Shot from the deadly level of a gun,
> Did murder her, as that name's cursed hand
> Murder'd her kinsman. O, tell me, friar, tell me,
> In what vile part of this anatomy
> Doth my name lodge? Tell me, that I may sack
> The hateful mansion. (III, iii, 102-08)

But though this echoes Juliet's other famous question and her insistence that a name is after all "nor hand, nor foot,/Nor arm, nor face," it is far different from "What's in a name?" in even its immediate implications. The trouble with Romeo's name here is not that it is a trivial attribute that raises accidental difficulties, but that "Romeo" now has a history, an inescapable reality of its own. It is the name of the man who has killed Tybalt; it is attached to a past and Romeo is responsible for it. It is Romeo who is banished for what Romeo has done. His anguish, though emotionally an

35

intensification of Juliet's in the balcony scene, is log-
ically an answer to her question. This, among other
things, is what's in a name.

Not only do names have a peculiar substantiality in
the play (they can murder, die, be torn; every tongue
that speaks "But Romeo's name speaks heavenly elo-
quence") but words themselves take on a namelike
intensity. That is, they take on, usually by repetition,
the importance and attributes of persons:

> Say thou but "I"
> And that bare vowel "I" shall poison more
> Than the death-darting eye of cockatrice.
> I am not I, if there be such an I;
> Or those eyes shut, that makes thee answer "I."[1]

> "... banished."
> That "banished," that one word "banished,"
> Hath slain ten thousand Tybalts.
>   (III, ii, 45-49, 112-14)

Here, as with "day" in IV, v,[2] the effect in the theater
is not to deepen the meaning of the word but at once
to strip the meaning away through endless repetition
and to give it a namelike life of its own.

As these examples suggest, naming is characteristically associated with separation in the play. It is no
accident that at the time of painful separation on the
morning after their marriage the lovers' aubade turns
on the name of a bird:

> It was the nightingale, and not the lark. . .

> It was the lark, the herald of the morn,
> No nightingale.   (III, v, 2-7)

---

[1] Restoring the Q₂ reading of "I" for "ay" in ll. 45, 48, and 49.
[2]   Most lamentable day, most woeful day,
           That ever, ever, I did yet behold!
           O day! O day! O day! O hateful day!
           Never was seen so black a day as this.
           O woeful day, O woeful day! (50-54)

They are passing from a night of sensual union to a day of exile. Night, as Mercutio has observed, is a time of free association, of fantastic invention, but day makes stricter demands upon our consciousness. When Romeo agrees to call the bird by some other name, Juliet must quickly admit that it is indeed the lark. The lovers relinquish the right to rename the world as they please; they must know the world's names for things if they wish to stay alive in it.

The play's everpresent thrust toward punning heightens our sense of the accepted meaning of words and of the rampant psychic energy that rises to break the meanings down. The wordplay makes its contribution as much by its quantity and irrepressibility as by its content. The puns are rapid and raw, emphasizing the suddenness and violence that is part of all punning, while the very process of punning raises issues that are central to the play. A pun is a sudden exchange of names, uniting objects we are not ordinarily allowed to unite, with a consequent release of energy, often violent and satisfying, and always satisfying to the extent that it is violent. It is something both terrible and lovely; we say "That's awful," when we mean "That's good." Romeo and Juliet themselves are like the components of a particularly good pun—natural mates whom authority strives to keep apart and whose union is not only violent but illuminating, since it transforms and improves the order it violates, though it is necessarily impermanent.

The fury of the pun is the fury of our submerged innocence; we play with words as Romeo and Juliet play with the lark and nightingale. Punning restores to us—under certain very narrow conditions, and for a brief interval—our freedom to change names and to make connections we have been taught to suppress, to invent language, to reconstitute the world as we please. *Romeo and Juliet* begins with a series of puns leading to a street brawl culminating in a dangerous mistake

37

(Benvolio, intending to restore order, draws his sword) that spreads the conflict to include nearly the entire company. The sequence is significant, for the energy of the pun, fully released in an organized society where names and rules are important, tends to be disastrous. Capulet and Montague lackeys lurk around the stage like forbidden meanings looking for an opportunity to discharge themselves. And at the level of responsible authority, the equivalent of the lackeys' idle brawling (or the overwhelming passion of the young lovers) is the capacity for instant and mistaken decision. From Benvolio's intervention in the opening street brawl to Romeo's suicide in the tomb, the play is a tissue of precipitous mistakes. Capulet hands a guest list to a servant who cannot read and the tragedy is initiated (significantly it is a list of names—all of which are read out —that is the villain). Mercutio's death is a mistake; and Romeo's error, like Capulet's and Benvolio's, enacts itself as a backfiring gesture, an action that—like a pun— subverts its manifest intention. Romeo's pathetic "I thought all for the best," rings in our ears when we see Lawrence and Capulet stricken by the lovers' death.

Counter to all the hasty and disastrous action of the play, there runs a surge of simple authoritative confidence, voiced at different times by almost every major character. The first scene ends with Romeo's assertion that he will always love Rosaline. As Romeo goes off, Capulet enters insisting that it will be easy to keep the peace. The juxtaposition of these two errors goes beyond simple irony; the encounter between confident assumption and the sudden event is one of the play's important motifs, just as the disparity between principle and practice is one of its recurrent themes. The Friar's first speech, for example, is often seen as a moralization of the action of *Romeo and Juliet*, and indeed there is a clear and effective dramatic connection between his homily and the action that surrounds it. The contrast between the night-time intensity of the scene immediately preceding, and the complacent tranquillity of Lawrence's reflections is obviously intended, and to further enforce the connection, he begins by moralizing the contrast:

> The grey-ey'd morn smiles on the frowning
>   night . . .
> And flecked darkness like a drunkard reels
> From forth day's path.   (II, iii, 1-4)

As he goes on, he seems to anticipate events that are to follow, but on closer inspection, his remarks are not precisely appropriate:

> Virtue itself turns vice, being misapplied;
> And vice sometime's by action dignified.
>   (21-22)

The first of these lines fits the lovers and much else in the play, but the second, though on the surface equally fitting, turns out to be harder to apply. Romeo is apparently acting in accordance with its teaching when he buys forbidden poison to use on himself, as is Capulet when he decides that a hasty marriage (which he has earlier roundly denounced) will rouse Juliet from her sorrows, or as the Nurse is when she advises Juliet to marry Paris. And Friar Lawrence certainly imagines he is taking a virtuous course when he offers poison to Juliet. By the play's end, of course, Lawrence's intervention has proved an example of virtue misapplied. The very confidence of his assertions becomes a source of disaster when he acts, and the very ease of his rhetoric is part of the texture of his actions. Friar Lawrence makes a strong bid to be the moral center of the play, but it is his bid that finally interests us more than his vision. Just as he shares a penchant for confidently interpreting events with Capulet, the Nurse, and Ro-

39

meo, among others, like them he has a disturbing capacity for guessing wrong.

At the end of the play Lawrence is pardoned. "We still have known thee for a holy man." The Friar deserves his reputation, and it is as necessary to society that he have his name for holiness as that he utter his sound and inappropriate *sententiae*. If he were not capable of making terrible mistakes, there would be no need of him. We must have friars and fathers, and all the system of responsibility that goes with naming, for the very reason that these figures fail in their responsibility: there is an energy in life that changes names, that breaks down the rules of language, of law, and even of luck.[3]

Romeo and Juliet bear the brunt of discovering this energy, and, like all tragic victims, they are isolated—even from each other—before they are destroyed. Characteristically, we remember them as separated: the drug comes between them in the final scene, earlier the balcony divides them; in the nightingale-lark scene they are together only at the moment of leave-taking. On all three occasions, the probable use of the stage serves to underline the strain that the effort toward contact demands of them—in Romeo's yearning upward toward the balcony, the perilous rope-ladder descent, the torches and crowbars breaking into the tomb. And of course there are always insistent voices—Mercutio and his friends, the Nurse, Paris, the watch—calling

[3] The play is famous for its long arias, of which there are two kinds. The speeches of the lovers are expressions of their isolation and desire; separated from each other, they speak at length. The Nurse, Mercutio, and Capulet, however, are given great bursts of speech in company; and the reaction of those around them is important. Their set-pieces are met with outcry; but they are carried away and will not stop. Each is a force in nature breaking into the expected or permissible flow of things; each imitates the impulsive action of the play, "of nothing first create"; each adds to the prevailing sense of impatience and irrepressible energy.

them away, repeating their names, threatening to interrupt them.

It is not fanciful to see their last scene in the tomb as suggestive of sexual union and of the sexual act. A battle takes place at the door, it is torn open—and on stage the barrier is finally only a curtain that gives easily enough after some bloodshed. It is also almost certainly the same inner stage or pavilion where Juliet has gone to bed on the eve of her wedding to Paris, and so it must remind the audience of that innocent chamber. (The curtains close as she falls on the bed, are opened in IV, v to show her apparently dead, and only open again, revealing her still prostrate, as Romeo breaks into the tomb.) The identification is given force by the new stream of wordplay that has entered since Tybalt's death, reversing the dominant pun of the play. Up to that point the language of combat has been transformed by punning into suggestions of sexual encounter ("Draw thy tool"); but in the concluding scenes, violent death is repeatedly described in terms of sex and the marriage festival. Romeo vows, "Well, Juliet, I will lie with thee tonight," meaning he will die; the lovers toast each other with poison ("Here's to my love," "This do I drink to thee"); and, in one of the great condensing images of the play, Juliet's beauty makes the "vault a feasting presence full of light." This last phrase catches up the play's repeated impressions of light and fire illuminating the night and suffuses the death of the lovers with a suggestion of their long-denied marriage banquet.

Romeo and Juliet, with its emphasis on language, young love, and the affectations and confusions of both, has clear affinities with the Shakespearean comedies of its period. Except for its fatalities, it follows the standard form of New Comedy. The two lovers are kept apart by a powerful external authority (some form of parental opposition is of course typical), and much of the action concerns their efforts to get around the obstacles placed in their path. Their ultimate union—in a marriage feast—results in a transformation of the society that has opposed them.

Like Romeo, Juliet, as she moves toward tragedy, is sometimes treated in a manner familiar from the early comedies: a sense of the "real" is produced by contrasting serious and superficial versions of the same situation or event. As Romeo progresses in seriousness from Rosaline to Juliet, so Juliet advances through at least three stages to her waking in the tomb. Lawrence sends her on her way with his usual cheery assurance, and even Romeo approaches his descent into the grave with a kind of boyish eagerness, but Juliet goes beyond them. Originally she shares their confident reading of the scene:

> . . . bid me go into a new-made grave
> And hide me with a dead man in his shroud,—
> Things that, to hear them told, have made me
>   tremble;
> And I will do it without fear or doubt.
>
> (IV, i, 84-87)

But her anticipatory vision of the tomb in IV, iii powerfully forecasts her actual fate:

> What if it be a poison, which the friar
> Subtly hath minist'red to have me dead . . .
> How if, when I am laid into the tomb,
> I wake before the time that Romeo
> Come to redeem me? . . .
> The horrible conceit of death and night,
> Together with the terror of the place,—
> As in a vault, an ancient receptacle,
> Where, for this many hundred years, the
>   bones
> Of all my buried ancestors are pack'd;
> Where bloody Tybalt, yet but green in earth,
> Lies fest'ring in his shroud. . .   (24-43)

"Fear and doubt" do afflict her, but it is even more notable that Juliet is the only one in the play who begins to guess what the final scene will be like.

In the tomb itself, Juliet continues to display her distinctive isolation and awareness. Her fate is given a final impressiveness by a gesture that carries on the special violence of the play. Shakespeare follows his source, Brooke's *The Tragical History of Romeus and Juliet*, in having Juliet commit suicide with Romeo's knife. But his Juliet, unlike Brooke's, first canvasses other ways to die—the poisoned cup, a kiss. These deaths, like Romeo's, are elegant, leave no mark upon the body, and have the comforting theatrical import of an easy transcendence of death—but they are not available to her; the impulsive pace of the action will not allow it. The watch is heard. She reaches for the dagger instead:

> This is thy sheath; there rust, and let me die.
> (v, iii, 170)

The death is messy, violent, sexual. It is interesting that Romeo's is the more virginal, and that Juliet's is the first in the play that has not been immediately caused by a misunderstanding.

Against the play's general background, its rapidly assembling crowds, its fevered busyness, its continual note of impatience and the quick violence of its encounters, the image that remains most strongly in our minds is not of the lovers as a couple, but of each as a separate individual grappling with internal energies that both threaten and express the self, energies for which language is inadequate but that lie at the root of language, that both overturn and enrich society. Touched by adult desire, the unsounded self bursts out with the explosive, subversive, dangerous energy of the sword, gunpowder, the plague; and every aspect of our experience of *Romeo and Juliet* in the theater engages us in this phenomenon—from the crude rush

43

of the brawling lackeys to the subliminal violence of the puns. We undergo, in a terrible condensation like the lightning-flash, the self-defining, self-immolating surge with which adolescence is left behind. As Juliet swiftly outgrows the comforts of the family circle, so Romeo moves far from the youthful packs that roam the streets of Verona, so many Adonises hunting and scorning. The lovers remain in the audience's minds in a typical pose and atmosphere, lights burning in the darkness, their names called, their farewells taken, each isolated in a moment of violent and enlightening desire.

IV

Falstaff Asleep

OUR BODY is both our history and our kingdom. We inherit it, we are responsible for it and to it, its boundaries are sacred, it tells a story we struggle to understand. Where the body is concerned, the career of "mature life" is a gradual failure of administration. We rule like disappointed tyrants, by fiats that prove ineffective. We chafe under its limitations and familiar ways. We are loving parents betrayed by the strength and weakness of our childish flesh, and at the same time its ambitious children, who cannot escape the ancestral tenement.

If all the nagging contradictions and avoidances common to familial life are present in our relations with our body, so are the grandeur and *folie* of national pride. We are by necessity the body's patriots. Indeed, to reverse for a moment what is by its very essence reversible, the emotion of patriotism would seem to be largely rooted in our emotions toward our parents and our body. "Give me life," the body cries, and self-indulgence and self-defense are the twin motors of patriotic fervor. Whatever our personal or political morality, there is a place in the depths of our being where we receive national and bodily conquests alike, with a flash of reassurance.

Falstaff's presence in the Henry IV plays guarantees that we cannot think long about politics without returning to the needs and achievements of the body. We are always eager for him to reappear, and welcome evidence of his good health even at the most inappropriate moments. Our attachment to him would seem to unbalance the drama, but we are aware that it is perfectly balanced—that the variety (especially in the first part) is held in an unusually elegant unity. And even though the plays' appeal to patriotism must be counted successful, it is curiously difficult to separate it from the appeal of the fat knight. Falstaff seems somehow to embody the English glory he clearly undermines. He is the genius of his drama in every sense. If he must be expelled—and he must, for the health of the nation—the comment of his doctor seems to the point: England may have more diseases than it knows, but "the water itself [is] a good healthy water."

Good government requires renunciation, but Falstaff is at home in *Henry IV* not simply because he has to be renounced. He has no politics; that is why he is central to these most political of plays. One of their effects is to enlarge our sense of government to the point where it interpenetrates with every phase of life. Not that we come to see political maneuvering or intention in every transaction, but rather that we become aware of the life of the state, as of the body, in a newly diverse and expansive way. Just as any heightened sense of the demands and delights of the body suggests how the state and its history are larger than any politics, so the notion of a "history" play in Shakespeare has been from his first efforts in the genre an inclusive, incorporative notion that tends to a teeming and full presentation of the body politic. If it is only through brilliant organization that the abundance of the Henry IV plays is buckled within the belt of rule, even our appreciation of their formal excellence reminds us how cunning good government needs to be.

In times of stress the health of the body, like that of the state, demands above all a profound awareness of one's interests. In Henry IV's England the great liability is shallowness. When Falstaff criticizes John of Lancaster for not being a drinker, for subsisting on thin potations, his critique has a political application, at least in part. John, he says, will never be the military man his brother is; he will not come to any proof. And

in a play in which the capacity to be various and flexible is important and associated both with political skill
and personal delight, the argument he uses is particularly significant. Drink, he explains, is necessary to a
rich and varied inner life:

A good sherris-sack hath a two-fold operation in it.
It ascends me into the brain; dries me there all the foolish and dull and crudy vapours which environ it; makes
it apprehensive, quick, forgetive, full of nimble, fiery,
and delectable shapes; which, delivered o'er to the
voice, the tongue, which is the birth, becomes excellent
wit. The second property of your excellent sherris is,
the warming of the blood. . . . It illumineth the face,
which as a beacon gives warning to all the rest of this
little kingdom, man, to arm; and then the vital com-
moners and inland petty spirits muster me all to their
captain, the heart, who, great and puff'd up with this
retinue, doth any deed of courage; and this valour
comes of sherris. (2 *Henry IV*, IV, iii, 103-122)

The contrast he makes between Hal and his brother is
accurate enough—though Falstaff is fatally unaware
that the richness of Hal's personality allows him to be,
among other things, quite as cold-blooded as any Lancaster—but it is John himself who reminds the rebels
how dangerous their lack of political depth has proved:

You are too shallow, Hastings, much too shallow,
To sound the bottom of the after-times.

Most shallowly did you these arms commence,
Fondly brought here and foolishly sent hence.
(2 *Henry IV*, IV, ii, 50-51, 118-19)

John of Lancaster is shallow, too, if only by comparison
with Hal, but his cruel characterization of the rebellion
he has broken by trickery is clearly meant to echo the
name of the guileless man Falstaff sets out to gull, just

47

as Shallow's judicial office reminds us of the unwob-
bling pivot of lawful authority under both Harrys, Falstaff's great enemy, the Lord Chief Justice. The vast
sweep and perfectly articulated parallelism of the plays
will have sensitized us to think of the fate of England
even in such charming backwaters as Shallow's or-
chard; we will not miss the overtones of Davy's comic
request of his master:

I grant your worship that he is a knave, sir; but yet,
God forbid, sir, but a knave should have some countenance at his friend's request. An honest man, sir, is
able to speak for himself, when a knave is not. I have
serv'd your worship truly, sir, this eight years; and if
I cannot once or twice in a quarter bear out a knave
against an honest man, I have but a very little credit
with your worship.   (2 *Henry IV*, v, i, 47-55)

Yet the dramatic point of this scene is not simply, or
even primarily that this is an instance of shallow justice, to be most sharply contrasted in the next scene by
the Chief Justice's stout defense of his having sent
Prince Hal himself to prison for offending "the majesty
and power of law and justice." The theatrical opportunities for charm—for merriment, the sense of abundance and happy, if dotty, busyness, even a degree of
winsomeness—are too great to be thrown away for bare
satire. Davy's request is delightful in its way, as Shallow's household is delightful and Falstaff, Pistol, Hotspur, and the Lady's song in Welsh are delightful. "Perhaps no author," Dr. Johnson writes, "has ever in two
plays afforded so much delight," and if we are to test
the secrets of the play's appeal, to try to arrive at the
nature and significance of the command it exerts over
our memory and imagination, we must not lose sight
of this central fact. The play is crammed with delight,
especially delight in abundance and overplus. The very

word makes us think of Falstaff, and Dr. Johnson's comment suggests that if Falstaff does not throw the play out of balance it is because the emotion with which we experience him is precisely what binds the play together and organizes our reaction to the whole. Delight is in effect the medium through which we perceive its actions, and our apprehension of such notions as shallowness, rebellion, or renunciation swims in the great stream of our delight.

Our delight in Falstaff is, to adopt a formula Eliot devised and applied to poetry, an emotion compounded out of many feelings.[1] Eliot's point—which lies behind so much of modern literary criticism—is nowhere more pertinent than in the theater. The feelings out of which the emotion in a lyric poem is composed may be described as feelings *about*, the investment of impulse in a rose, a typewriter, Spinoza, another person, etc. In the theater, by contrast, our primary feelings are feelings *toward* what we see on the stage, particularly toward the actors. We don't think about a rose; we see a rose. More important, we see an actor, a man of medium height, say, with dark hair and thick hands, smelling a rose. Our emotion is composed of impulses toward real persons and the objects and feelings they handle. The audience's response at any time is built up out of a number of active, specific, and ongoing human relationships. Each has a coloration, it is true, not quite like any relation we enter into outside the theater, but the activity of the impulse is the same. The scenes at Justice Shallow's, for example, bring into play a range of related responses. (1) Especially in v, iii, there is the feeling of festivity. Shallow's estate is abundant and well-run. There are old men here, as there are all over England, but here they are harmless and hospitable. The word in v, iii is "merry":

[1] "Tradition and the Individual Talent," *Selected Essays*, 3rd ed. (London, 1951), pp. 18ff.

49

CHAPTER IV

SILENCE

"Do nothing but eat, and make good cheer,
And praise God for the merry year,
When flesh is cheap and females dear,
And lusty lads roam here and there
     So merrily,
And ever among so merrily."

FALSTAFF

There's a merry heart! . . .

SHALLOW

Be merry, Master Bardolph; and, my little
   soldier there, be merry.

SILENCE

[*Singing.*] "Be merry, be merry. . ."

                                        (18-35)

But though we share in this version of Merry England
and wish for it to be prolonged (must Master Silence go
to bed?), there is (2) something valedictory about the
old men at play, something faint and thin about Silence's bursts of song and Shallow's reminiscences. At
the same time (3) they are innocent and easily ruled,
as Shallow is by Davy and Falstaff and as Silence is by
drink. They are all too ready to rush to London and
abandon themselves, in their feeble way ("lusty Shallow"), to the life of the senses, ready, as we know, to
be swindled. We long to protect them even as we long
to see them fooled.

Our experience of Falstaff is likewise the sum of
many experiences developed over many scenes, and at
almost any instant a multitude of feelings will be en-
twined. Some of the most constant elements, however,
rather parallel the chord of feeling awakened by the
Shallow scenes. There is of course (1) the impression
of the abundant revel in which we are eager to participate. We are always happy to see Falstaff back on the
stage. At the same time, there is (2) the pathos of Falstaff's rejection by the Prince, and (3) the sense that

the revel properly must end, that Falstaff's individual play must cease so that the full pleasure of *the* play may be achieved, that Falstaff will have to be put down to end the disorder of England.[2]

In the matter of Falstaff's rejection, certain misconceptions need to be dealt with. The pathos of this event does not derive from its being unexpected, but rather from its inevitability. If Falstaff's banishment were in any way a surprise it might be shocking, but not pathetic—any more than if Olivia were to turn Toby Belch out in the final scene of *Twelfth Night*. Toby and Falstaff are very different, but the root of the difference lies in Toby's consanguinity. He is part of the family; he belongs. His wit is simply an expression of his personality, while Falstaff's is at least in part a device for keeping in the good graces of the Prince, on whom he can make no permanent claim. In spite of her threats, we know that Olivia will never abandon Toby. We always know—at any rate, we should know—that Hal will never keep Falstaff on.

If there is any surprise in the rejection, it comes about for two reasons: first, the thoroughness and bleakness of the gesture; second, and more important, Falstaff's foolish confidence in the security of his position. It is the latter which makes the pathos finally so intense. From the first, Falstaff's situation is clear. It is not merely that we are "prepared" for the rejection; we are intended to expect it. The distinction is important. In response to more than a century of senti-

[2] Running through both parts there is a tension between improvisation and scriptedness which corresponds to the tension between comedy and history, between Falstaff and the serious world, between clown and playwright, play and *the* play, between what we want of Falstaff and what must happen to him. In one sense Hal is on the side of scriptedness, but he also recognizes the virtues of improvisation in a scripted world (as in Part One, II, iv and Part Two, IV, v). Hotspur by contrast is too scripted for his own safety.

51

mentalization, modern criticism has been at pains to prove that Falstaff's rejection is a blemish neither on the Prince nor on the play. The evidence as to his viciousness, his lineage as the Vice in the Morality tradition, the analogies the play draws between Falstaff and the rebels, has all been tallied up, quite correctly and irrefutably. Perhaps because of its polemical origin, however, this line of discussion has tended to misplace Shakespeare's emphasis. Hal's "I know you all" soliloquy, his "I do, I will," the mockery and guying of Falstaff that begins with Hal's cutting reply to the old knight's inoffensive opening line, are not introduced as "preparation" for the rejection, in the sense that they are included to make it comprehensible when it comes, to innoculate us, as it were, against an excessive outbreak of sympathy for Falstaff at the play's end. The information is not designed to be kept buried until the instant of rejection. This is not the *Famous Victories of Henry V*, where the drinking and drabbing Prince of Wales is metamorphosed into a proper young ruler overnight. After "I know you all" (and very likely even earlier) we are meant to know that Hal already understands the discipline required by his destiny, and assents to it. The pathos of Falstaff's rejection is a motif that runs through the two plays, and it builds upon our certainty that, in some form, it must finally occur. This is something any performance makes us aware of, but we are likely to discount it as a product of irrelevant sophistication, of "knowing how the play will end." Shakespeare's audience knew too, and they too, one might guess, felt the touching silliness as well as the splendid extravagance in Falstaff's:

Master Shallow, my Lord Shallow,—be what thou wilt; I am Fortune's steward—get on thy boots. We'll ride all night. O sweet Pistol! Away, Bardolph! Come, Pistol, utter more to me; and withal devise something to do thyself good. Boot, boot, Master Shallow! I know

the young king is sick for me. Let us take any man's
horses; the laws of England are at my commandment.

(2 *Henry IV*, v, iii, 135-43)

The point is not so much that he is rejected at the
end, but that from the beginning he has been a candi-
date for rejection. Falstaff's dangerous influence on Hal
is only apparent, and those—like Hal's father—who are
taken in by it are shallower in the arts of government
than the Prince. To Hal, Falstaff is no more than a
cloud, a "contagious" one, to be sure, but the contagion
does not extend to the "sun" who can part the clouds
at will. Hal, the supreme governor, is a master of ap-
pearances, as even the scene with poor Francis indicates. Hal bewilders Francis with contradictory commands and obscure appeals to rebellion and self-
interest:

PRINCE

Francis, darest thou be so valiant as to play the coward
with thy indenture and show it a fair pair of heels and
run from it?

FRANCIS

O Lord, sir, I'll be sworn upon all the books in England,
I could find in my heart—

POINS

[*Within.*] Francis!

FRANCIS

Anon, sir. . . .

PRINCE

Wilt thou rob this leathern jerkin, crystal-button, not-
pated, agate-ring, puke-stocking, caddis-garter, smooth-
tongue, Spanish-pouch,—

FRANCIS

O Lord, sir, who do you mean?

PRINCE

Why, then, your brown bastard is your only drink; for
look you, Francis, your white canvas doublet will sully.
In Barbary, sir, it cannot come to so much.

FRANCIS

What, sir?

POINS

[*Within.*] Francis!

PRINCE

Away, you rogue! dost thou not hear them call?
Here they both call him; the drawer stands amazed, not
knowing which way to go.

(*1 Henry IV*, II, iv, 51-89)

Francis here is a foil to Falstaff, who in the long bout
that follows cannot be so easily manipulated. The scene
also shows Hal's restless skill at impersonation. He has
already succeeded in being taken for a thief and passed
muster as "sworn brother to a leash of drawers." Soon
he is to imitate Hotspur and act the part of his father
in a play extempore. When Poins asks him why he has
played his joke on Francis, Hal's only answer is that
he is "now of all humours that have showed themselves
humours since the old days of goodman Adam to the
pupil age of this present twelve o'clock at midnight"
(104-107); he then slips quickly into his imitation of
Hotspur. He is ready to try all sorts of roles. In a sense,
only Falstaff comes near Hal as a player of roles, as
only Hotspur—and later the Lord Chief Justice—comes
near him in firmness of purpose. Francis is totally lacking in both. Like Shallow and his household, he is
wavering and simple and easily imposed on. People
are like that (even the rebels); the nation needs to be
led. The rejection of Falstaff is more than a symbolic
act that completes for the audience a portrait of Hal's
character as ideal king. It is a political act, a public
event, whose effect corresponds to the program laid
out by the Prince in his first soliloquy. When the newly
crowned Henry V speaks of his "former self," of his
"riots" and the "thing" he was, he seems to refer not so
much to the rather careful if fun-loving young man we
have known for nine acts, but to the scapegrace of

popular legend, to his "public image" in fact. The former self he is repudiating is the character people have imagined for him, not one he has actually deserved. But Shakespeare knew as early as *Lucrece* that, in politics, dramatic mutations of the self are often more publicly significant than privately real.

At the moment of Falstaff's rejection, then, we find ourselves observing Henry from a slightly altered angle. The point of view is not entirely new; we have experienced something like it in the Prince's first interview with his father in Part One, and it has mingled with our more familiar way of seeing him in the great scene with the crown at his father's bedside. But now for the first time it is decisive and paramount. When Henry publicly renounces his public character, he is operating in a new sphere. He is speaking not quite to us but to his audience on stage, for effect. He is performing—but not as he did in the Boar's Head Tavern, out of a spontaneous, self-delighting impulse. He "plays" now for higher stakes. Though we may approve of his actions and his sentiments, we cannot help noticing the political usefulness of his performance.

Falstaff is always at Hal's mercy, and we love him for the way he stretches the limits of his situation and gets away with it; it is an aspect of his fatness. At the end of the Boar's Head Tavern scene, when it is learned that the Sheriff and his watch are at the door hunting Falstaff, he hides behind the arras while the Prince persuades the Sheriff to leave. The curtain is then drawn back, and Falstaff is revealed, asleep and "snorting like a horse." The Prince goes through his pockets. Falstaff sleeps on for twenty lines as the scene concludes. The episode is memorable, funny, famous even among familiar quotations ("O monstrous! but one half-pennyworth of bread to this intolerable deal of sack!"), and—perhaps because Falstaff cannot speak—suggests with a fascinating strength the intensity and complexity of our attachment to him. Falstaff asleep is the man we have seen wildly and ingeniously awake moments before, and we look forward to the moment he will rise again. His belches and snorts undoubtedly have more life in them than an army of tapsters. Francis's actions belong to the comedy of mechanism; he has responded to the Prince's commands like an automaton. Falstaff's, even asleep, belong to the comedy of irrepressibility; he is doing what he wants in the most unlikely of circumstances. And yet perhaps because he is asleep, certain other strands of our feeling toward him are allowed to take on new prominence. The contrast with the long, energetic, increasingly fantastic comic scene that has been interrupted, the relative stillness, our new awareness that it is late at night, our growing certainty that a decisive return to the great world of politics and combat is imminent, all these tend to heighten whatever is protective and elegiac in our response. It is a good scene to meditate on.

Falstaff at this moment seems not only grandly self-indulgent and indifferent to crisis but particularly vulnerable. The Prince stands over him; Falstaff's life is in his hands in more ways than one. He has promised the Sheriff that the fat knight will make good his thefts. He makes Peto read aloud the ludicrous facts of Falstaff's internal economy. Falstaff's utter relaxation is enviable, his snorting and belching delightfully irreverent, but the guard that has been up so splendidly throughout the long tavern scene is down and the soft belly is exposed. We feel drawn to him and we see how easily we can hurt him; we know now that the wars have begun, that he won't do as he is. Falstaff must suffer. He must submit to the indignities of realism, of number and measure. Today his appetites are converted into arithmetic ("Item, Sack, two gallons . . . 5s. 8d."); tomorrow he must lead a charge of foot. ("I know his death will be a march of twelve-score. The money shall be paid back again with advantage.") We know that Falstaff will respond resourcefully; he is far from finished. But we have always known that finished he eventually must be.

Falstaff is not only endlessly inventive and delightful, audacious and dangerous, but vulnerable. This is also true about the things for which he comes to stand—our sensuality and our impulse to anarchy. The tenderness, broad humor, and absurdity that are mixed in this tableau come close to the mystery of Falstaff—or more correctly the mystery of the play, for our emotion here includes Hal, whose stance is the already familiar one of authority and detachment, and whose heroic career is plainly about to begin. The Prince of our reason stands over the attractive, grotesque, audacious, pathetically vulnerable body of our sensuality—an image for one of the many selves inside us, indeed for more than one—a sleeping child that we will have to punish, the silly, dying father we are destined to displace.

V

Henry V
The Strain of Rule

Henry v is a play of great addresses. They make for a vital bond of pleasure that joins us to the play; it is absolutely essential to any satisfying production that the actors be capable of all these speeches demand. The grand declamations of both King and Chorus induce a kind of theatrical kinesthesia not yet considered in this volume; they make us want to act. I doubt that anyone can read the play through without reading some of these speeches aloud—and, if at all possible, loudly. They are display arias for the commanding actor; they stimulate us to share his noticeable effort, to be aware of the glory and labor involved in making authoritative sounds. They carry with them, in the most patent and seductive form, the pleasures, the rewarding effort of persuasive, masterful public performance. Their verse is wonderfully suited to the accents of a man speaking to a crowd, a confident man, practiced in exertion but working hard, raising his voice, stilling and exhorting the group around him. Their content, too, seems to echo their physical appeal. Significantly, all but one of the half-dozen famous speeches of the play have in common a concern for encouraging their hearers to make some kind of demanding effort, whether of action, feeling, or imagination. These speeches insist on what is strenuous, and *Henry V*'s dominant atmosphere is of strenuous activity. The play communicates a sense not exactly or not primarily of strain, but of straining effort, of life that is arduous, exigent, and sometimes exhausting.

Once it is recognized that the Chorus sounds very much like the King, much of the play's method becomes clear. Like Henry, the Chorus is a man whose job is to rouse his hearers to unusual effort. The straining note is struck from the start, and may well be the primary reason for the Chorus's existence, since none of the theories ordinarily advanced to account for Shakespeare's unparalleled reliance on the device is satisfactory. Elsewhere he uses a chorus to provide a background or set a mood (*Romeo and Juliet*) or to direct our attention to a special aspect of the scene to follow (2 *Henry IV*). But nowhere else does he use it to call attention to the inadequacies of his stage, which is of course no more inadequate to this story than to the material of the other histories. Here, however, the notion of inadequacy is insisted upon, as is the effort we must put forth to make up for it:

> O for a Muse of fire, that would ascend
> The brightest heaven of invention,
> A kingdom for a stage, princes to act,
> And monarchs to behold the swelling scene!
> (Prologue, 1-4)

The playwright and the resources of his stage are deficient, but so are we, and we are asked to perform all kinds of brain-work to convert the work of the actors into a convincing spectacle.

At the same time, the Chorus develops a complementary sense of the size and energy of the subject, both of which are pictured as being held in with difficulty, barely restrained or contained:

> . . . at his heels,
> Leash'd in like hounds, should famine,
>   sword, and fire
> Crouch for employment.

> Can this cockpit hold
> The vasty fields of France? Or may we cram
> Within this wooden O the very casques
> That did affright the air at Agincourt?
>
> Suppose within the girdle of these walls
> Are now confin'd two mighty monarchies,
> Whose high upreared and abutting fronts
> The perilous narrow ocean parts asunder.[1]
> (Prologue, 6-8, 11-14, 19-22)

It is a "swelling" scene—and the epithet not only means "magnificent" but carries the modern meaning (common in Shakespeare's day) as well; some distending energy within the scene threatens to break it apart. We are asked not to imagine many men where we see one but to "divide" one man "into a thousand parts." As the Chorus says in his second appearance, the project we are engaged in is to "force a play."[2]

Introducing the third act, the Chorus returns to the charge. The effort of the enterprise described is caught in the contrast between the delicacy of the sails and the huge vessels they move through the water, and the effort is echoed in the sound and movement of the verse:

> Behold the threaden sails,
> Borne with th' invisible and creeping wind,
> Draw the huge bottoms through the furrowed sea,
> Breasting the lofty surge. (10-13)

The audience is enjoined to strain its minds, to apply the same effort to imagining the war. Commands to "suppose" and "think" give way to "Follow, follow," "Grapple your minds to sternage of this navy," and

---

[1] Here there is a sense not only of the danger of the ocean, but of a fragile barrier between two threatening hugenesses.

[2] Dover Wilson's suggestion that "force" is to be understood in the culinary sense of "stuff" is interesting in this connection (New Cambridge Edition, 1947, p. 132).

"Work, work." The Chorus continues to remind us that this is not a battlefield, not an ocean, but merely a theater. Its soaring language, like the effort of imagination it enjoins, seems to be part of the struggle to overcome the limits of performance. The firing off of "chambers" in the theater—an effect repeated in the following scene—adds to the sensation of stupendous energies at work. Here and in other choruses we seem to hear continual reverberation—the womby earth being trampled by horses, ordnance going off, armorers busily hammering. Echoes, loud sounds, and hollow chambers are regularly referred to. In the fourth chorus, the universe is a "wide vessel" filled first by night and low sounds, then by the clang of armorers, cock-crow, and the approaching clamor of battle. There are descriptions of horses, too, by the Chorus and the French nobles, that help sustain this aural atmosphere:

> Steed threatens steed, in high and boastful neighs
> Piercing the night's dull ear;
>> (IV, Prologue, 10-11)

> When I bestride him, I soar, I am a hawk; he trots the air; the earth sings when he touches it;
>> (III, vii, 15-17)

> Mount them, and make incision in their hides,
> That their hot blood may spin in English eyes,
> And dout them with superfluous courage, ha!
>> (IV, ii, 9-11)

Our ears are assaulted and roused to gratified awareness by the repeated suggestion of vast spaces to be filled by energetic outbursts, by the strain of producing the energy, and by the energy itself straining to be set free.

I have suggested that the figure of the Chorus rousing the audience to cooperation and excitement is rather like the figure of Henry addressing his men. Just as the Chorus's speeches emphasize effort and strain and the making of much out of little, so throughout the play we are aware of the effort and strain of leading an army, of making a kingdom bigger, of turning a man into a soldier, and indeed of turning a man into a king. Immediately after the Chorus has begun Act III by urging us to follow, grapple, and work, and with the "devilish cannon" still echoing in our ears, the King enters. His men carry scaling ladders; we are in the midst of battle. Henry V, like the chorus before him, exhorts his hearers to make a strenuous imaginative effort; he asks them to transform themselves, to change their size, shape, and strength, to eke out the performance with their minds:

> Stiffen the sinews, summon up the blood,
> Disguise fair nature with hard-favour'd rage;
> Then lend the eye a terrible aspect;
> Let it pry through the portage of the head
> Like the brass cannon; let the brow o'erwhelm it
> As fearfully as doth a galled rock
> O'erhang and jutty his confounded base,
> Swill'd with the wild and wasteful ocean.
> Now set the teeth and stretch the nostril wide,
> Hold hard the breath, and bend up every spirit
> To his full height.   (i, 7-17)

The soldier's task of preparation is described as a violent muscular contortion. He must strain his muscles so that his eye pries through his face till it sticks out like a cannon—and of course it is a brass cannon, with all the sense of metallic echoing sound this brings in. "On, on," he cries to the troops, as the Chorus has cried "Follow, follow" and "Work, work" to us. Physical limitation overcome by supreme effort is Henry's theme here, and it is also the method of his speech, which requires a great physical effort from the speaker. It makes a splendid noise; it is full of demanding emphases and syntactical elaborations. From a vocal standpoint, the speech is a remarkable athletic exercise, and a directly gratifying one for the actor who can manage it. Theatrical tradition leaves no doubt of the speech's power to excite and charm an audience—a point which needs to be stressed in the light of some influential— and useful—modern criticism. It is misleading to conclude from the extremity of its verbal figures that the speech is meant to project a feeling of the grotesque or unpleasant. To do so, to find as Traversi does that there is a "strong flavor of artificiality . . . something forced, incongruous, even slightly absurd"[3] in the speech is, I think, to consider the words out of theatrical context, without concern for the acting opportunities, the physical presence and rhythms of the scene. True, the actor runs a terrific obstacle course on the way to his final self-assertive shout:

Cry, "God for Harry! England and Saint George!"

If he allows the absurd or incongruous to emerge along the way, he will fail to negotiate it. One might say of a running track lined with hurdles and patches of water, "There is a strong flavor here of falling flat on one's face," but the obstacles are there precisely to celebrate the virtues of those who do not fall flat, and to clothe their skills in wonder.

This is the play in which Falstaff dies; and the scenes—early in the play—in which we learn of his death and see what his friends are now like, help to

[3] *An Approach to Shakespeare*, 2d ed. (New York, 1956), p. 39. I must in fairness point out that Traversi also uses the word "strain" to describe the flavor, but, I think, in a different sense from what I intend. I have in mind the effort of the body against limitation, the effort of an athlete going full-out. He may well be extending himself beyond his normal capacity, and such an effort may in time take its toll, on others if not on himself. It certainly implies some estrangement from ordinary life in terms of the training required and the stress regularly endured. But it is successful effort, and not muscle-cramp or hernia.

set its tone. A number of critics have noticed the element of darkness or chill which the treatment of Falstaff contributes to *Henry V*, and all may at least agree that it does add to the sense of strain creeping into its genuinely heroic occasions.

The opening scenes of Act II show us first Hal's old friends and then some of his new friends—the traitors Scroop, Grey, and Cambridge. Scroop was Henry's "bedfellow (ii, 8) . . . [who] didst bear the key of all my counsels . . . knew'st the very bottom of my soul (96-97)." His new friends betray him (or like Canterbury and Ely deal with him on a political level where intimacy can only be an illusion or a danger); his old friends think he has betrayed Falstaff. The comedy of Pistol, Nym, and Bardolph of course echoes the serious action ("On, on, on, on, on! To the breach, to the breach!" shouts Bardolph as Hal's Harfleur speech concludes), but it also develops the sense of strain. Nym and Pistol are cowards who feign different kinds of toughness. What we laugh at are the kinds of effort they make in doing so. Nym pretends to a tight-lipped laconic ominousness:

I cannot tell. Things must be as they may. Men may sleep, and they may have their throats about them at that time; and some say knives have edges.
(II, i, 22-25)

Pistol, on the other hand, is like Henry and the Chorus, a great vocal artist and exhorter. His speeches even impress Fluellen for a time. Pistol and Nym's performances are at least good enough to take each other in; they frighten one another thoroughly in II, i. Theirs is not the effortless improvisation of their former leader, but a perpetual straining to perform. Falstaff is shifty and always ready to retreat, but one never feels he is seriously concealing his real self. He is his facade, and his bravura is always accompanied by a wink. Pistol and Nym cower inside their affectations.

Falstaff's old gang forms a particularly scabrous appendage to an army that grows increasingly weak and ragged as the play progresses. There are a number of references to its condition, and at one point the stage directions are unusually explicit (I give the Folio wording):

Enter the King and his poor Soldiers.
(III, vi, 91)

In part this points up the greatness of Henry's victory at Agincourt. It allows us, too, to see Henry as the shepherd of a small enfeebled flock. But the plight of the troops also helps sustain a kind of ratty counterpoint to the strenuous music of triumph. Consider the following sequence of exhortations, all of which are heard within some 74 lines:

CHORUS
Follow, follow!
Grapple your minds etc. . . .
Work, work . . .
(III, Prologue, 17ff.)

K. HENRY
Unto the breach . . .
Follow your spirit, and upon this charge
Cry, "God for Harry! England and Saint George!"
(III, i, 1-34)

BARDOLPH
On, on, on, on, on! To the breach, to the breach!
(III, ii, 1-2)

FLUELLEN
Up to the breach, you dogs! Avaunt, you cullions!
(III, ii, 21-22)

Bardolph's is already an unheroic parody in the familiar vein of the Elizabethan comic underplot, but Fluellen's echo cuts deeper. We are reminded that there are

65

men who have to be scolded and perhaps whipped into battle. "You dogs!" is finally but a basic-English translation of what the King calls his soldiers:

I see you stand like greyhounds in the slips.
(III, i, 31)

It is not only famine, sword, and fire that "leash'd in like hounds . . . crouch for employment" at King Harry's heels.

It is this picture of the army, set against the more exalting music of grand effort, that will be in the audience's minds as the fourth act begins with its scenes of the King moving among his men. These encounters turn out differently from what Henry expects, and, more important, from what the audience has been led to expect. The Chorus, ending its night-piece, seems to prepare us very fully for what is to come:

For forth he goes and visits all his host,
Bids them good morrow with a modest smile,
And calls them brothers, friends, and country-
    men.
Upon his royal face there is no note
How dread an army hath enrounded him;
. . . every wretch, pining and pale before,
Beholding him, plucks comfort from his looks.
A largess universal like the sun
His liberal eye doth give to every one,
Thawing cold fear, that mean and gentle all
Behold, as may unworthiness define,
A little touch of Harry in the night.
(32-47)

The problem is that the King does not do this—at least in the scenes that follow. It could perhaps be argued that the Chorus is simply describing what the King has been doing up to now, but the Chorus sounds as if it is providing an introduction rather than a bridge, and the scene starts out as if we were indeed about to see the kind of thing the Chorus has described. On the basis of sound generalship alone, to say nothing of what we have just been told, we might expect that Harry would want to go round the camp, *as the King,* and say a few good words to individual soldiers, as he does to Sir Thomas Erpingham,[4] reassuring them, with a judicious use of the common touch, that the King has their interests at heart and is a good fellow to boot, "a bawcock and a heart of gold," as Pistol would say.

Instead, the King disguises himself. The effect of his subsequent conversation on the soldiers cannot fairly be called encouraging; it is disconcerting at best. He tries, in the character of a private man, to draw them out about his character as a king, and his trouble seems to be that he cannot maintain both roles simultaneously. Even with Pistol, things go a little oddly. We do not get the expected joke, patented in *Henry IV*—and consequently what Shakespeare's audience would be waiting for—of the rogue behaving badly when he thinks the Prince isn't watching. Pistol does not criticize Hal as Falstaff does when the Prince is disguised as a waiter in 2 *Henry IV.* But there is something out of key and embarrassing about his praise of Henry, if only because he insists too vulgarly upon the King's human qualities.

With Bates, Court, and Williams, Henry insists at length on the humanity of the King:

For, though I speak it to you, I think the King is but a man, as I am. The violet smells to him as it does to me; the element shows to him as it doth to me; all his senses have but human conditions. His ceremonies laid by, in his nakedness he appears but a man; and though his affections are higher mounted than ours, yet, when they stoop, they stoop with the like wing.

<hr>

[4] Even here, Erpingham seems more to cheer the King up than vice versa.

Therefore, when he sees reason of fears as we do, his fears, out of doubt, be of the same relish as ours are . . .
(IV, i, 104-114)

This is in service of a rather special argument:

yet, in reason, no man should possess him with any appearance of fear, lest he, by showing it, should dishearten his army.   (114-17)

In other words, because he is a man the King is susceptible to fear, but because he is a king we must conspire to keep him from being afraid.

He sounds out the men on their feelings toward the King and passionately (even comically) defends himself when he feels they put too great a responsibility upon him. They accept his argument that the King is not to blame if a soldier dies with sins on his head, and they show a ready loyalty:

WILLIAMS
'Tis certain, every man that dies ill, the ill upon his own head, the King is not to answer it.
BATES
I do not desire he should answer for me; and yet I determine to fight lustily for him.   (197-201)

Nevertheless, Henry seems unsatisfied. The soldiers' loyalty to the public man is unquestionable, but now he asks them for a favorable judgment on the King's private attitudes:

HENRY
I myself heard the King say he would not be ransom'd.
(202-203)

Like any sensible soldier, however, Williams knows that political calculation lies behind any public pronouncement:

68

Ay, he said so [he replies], to make us fight cheerfully; but when our throats are cut, he may be ransom'd, and we ne'er the wiser.

Earlier, informed by Henry that the King's cause is just, Williams has said, "That's more than we know," and now he maintains the position. The soldiers can know the King only as loyal subjects, not as peers or brothers. But Henry, dangerously, keeps at it:

HENRY
If I live to see it, I will never trust his word after.

WILLIAMS
You pay him then. That's a perilous shot out of an elder-gun, that a poor and a private displeasure can do against a monarch! . . . You'll never trust his word after! Come, 'tis a foolish saying.

HENRY
Your reproof is something too round. I should be angry with you, if the time were convenient.

(207-219)

The scene is remarkably imagined. Henry is in understandable difficulties, yet we cannot feel entirely in sympathy with him. He is asking too much. Now he is offended because Williams has spoken to him, the King, as he would to a private man. Henry has tried to appeal to the men both as a king and as a man who is not the King. It is unfair, and Williams will properly criticize him for it later:

Your Majesty came not like yourself. You appear'd to me but as a common man . . . and what your Highness suffer'd under that shape, I beseech you take it for your own fault and not mine.

(IV, viii, 53-57)

Henry's encounter with the soldiers prompts his one soliloquy, the speech on ceremony. Ceremony may be all a king has to set him off from other men, but we

69

scarcely need even Henry's deeply troubled recollec-
tion of Richard II in the prayer that follows to be reminded how great a difference ceremony makes, and
what a change in the quality of one's being it demands.
A king is not simply his role; his power and authority
do not flow directly from his person, as Richard, tragically, tried to insist. Neither, however, is a king simply
a man like other men, no matter how attractive and
at times politically useful the pretense may be. The
demands of office change a man. A king is not a man
like other men—but he is a man, and his humanity
consists in this: he must pay the price of his role.

The achievement of the play—the fact that with all
its ironies it remains great patriotic drama—lies with
its ability to project the glory of the ruler in a way that
is true to—indeed depends upon—the price of his role.
In the St. Crispin's Day address, for example, we are
stirred, certainly, by the way Henry meets the challenge of the moment and rallies his men, but our ses-
sions with the Chorus and the army have made us
sensitive to the fact that his speech, like the rejection
of Falstaff in 2 *Henry IV*, is a performance and not a
revelation of some previously unsounded self. It is in
part an attempt to deal with the cynicism he has met
in the night. When the King steps forward with,
"What's he that wishes so?" and claims that every
man who fights that day will be his brother, we are
thrilled. But we are thrilled because he is brilliantly
meeting a political challenge that has been spelled out
for us—as earlier he met the challenge of the tennis
balls. It is a moment when he must respond to the
unspoken needs of his men, and we respond to his
success as we do when a political leader we admire
makes a great campaign speech: we love him for his
effectiveness. The King is speaking *ex officio*, and if he
calls himself Harry, this is not because he is a man like
other men, speaking merely out of personal conviction
and desire. He is, rather, projecting an "image"—the

hero as good fellow (like "Ike" or "Jack" or "Bobby"). It has been developed for a purpose, and the King must rely on his muse, must place a strain on his imagination, himself, and his hearers—just as the play, according to the Chorus, must place a strain on us.

The actor's problem in this scene is, above all, that of being convincing as a leader. Interpretation, even technique, do not present primary difficulties. Performing convincingly is both the actor's and the character's greatest problem here. The speech is one in which Henry reveals not himself (in the manner of Junius Brutus, Richard III, or Juliet), but his abilities. We experience the moment of patriotism with a shock of approval rather than recognition.

In the battle that follows, we do not see any heroic combat. Beyond Pistol's craven bargaining with his prisoner, our only knowledge of the battle is by report— with one exception, and this involves the French prisoners, whose wretchedness, like that of the English army earlier, is forced upon us. The Folio stage direction for IV, vi reads, *"Enter the King and his train, with Prisoners."* The scene ends with Henry's command:

> The French have reinforc'd their scatter'd men.
> Then every soldier kill his prisoners;
> Give the word through.

Presumably the prisoners on stage are included in the order. In the next scene the slaughter is repeated, once more before our eyes. So the only bloodletting we experience directly is of the nastiest kind. Modern productions usually introduce a silent scene that shows the French killing the boys in the English camp—and often banish at least some of the English throat-cutting from the stage. But this is not true to Shakespeare. While his script allows us to comprehend that Henry's action is in some sense justified (like the invasion itself), we *feel* it at this point only as a blood-chilling fact.

71

Like Henry we have been schooled throughout the tetralogy in the renunciations and exertions demanded of the ideal king, and in the treatment of the prisoners on stage we are made to feel, as Henry does, the ashes in the mouth of all political glory.

We seem to be let off easily at the end. The charm of the wooing scene—which has proved irresistible to actors and audiences in spite of a long tradition of solemn critical disapproval—derives from the very spectacle of the King being a private man, both in his engaging awkwardness with Katharine, and in his playing in a plain and personal way with political ideas:

KATHARINE

Is it possible dat I should love de enemy of France?

HENRY

No; it is not possible you should love the enemy of France, Kate; but, in loving me, you should love the friend of France; for I love France so well that I will not part with a village of it.　　(v, ii, 178-83)

The prose, by contrast to the strenuous rhetoric of the play's verse, suggests the personal as opposed to the public. It is as if, after all the hardships, exertions, renunciations, and successes of the war, the King were now free to play the man, if only briefly.

It may seem surprising that the Hal of *Henry IV*, who was so adept at playing roles, should be at all heavy-footed here, and it is his apparent awkwardness, his exaggerated lack of polish that has most troubled critics (Tillyard calls him a "lubberly wooer"[5]). But this is unfair to the scene as it is written, and as it can be played by the actor who takes full advantage of its opportunities. For the King's awkwardness is never really out of control. He can strike the note of smooth and persuasive gallantry when he pleases:

[5] *Shakespeare's History Plays* (New York, 1947), p. 311.

Fair Katharine, and most fair,
Will you vouchsafe to teach a soldier terms
Such as will enter at a lady's ear
And plead his love-suit to her gentle heart?
(98-101)

and he can translate his public authority into seductive
energy, mixing force and grace:

O Kate, nice customs curtsy to great kings. Dear
Kate, you and I cannot be confined within the weak list
of a country's fashion. We are the makers of manners,
Kate; and the liberty that follows our places stops the
mouth of all find-faults, as I will do yours, for uphold-
ing the nice fashion of your country in denying me a
kiss; therefore, patiently and yielding.
(293-300)

The actor who plays Henry as genuinely embarrassed
in this scene will cheapen his comic effects and quickly
exhaust them. The point is that the King really has to
play at being the man; he is in a sense affecting a "humanity" perfectly appropriate to his position and his
audience (it is certainly well-calculated to impress
Katharine). His "private" life is as much a performance
as his speech on Crispin's Day.

This helps to explain why such an ending can be
deeply satisfying—not only pleasing in itself, but the
right note of mirth to cap the play. We are left with few
of the tragic reflections that pursue Henry when he
plays the man with Bates and Williams, though the
references to Henry VI in both the wooing scene and
the epilogue keep our contentment from going slack.
Though its gaiety is appropriate to Henry's moment of
success, the scene is fully consistent with the essential
impulse of the play—the effort of greatness, both what
it is like to make the effort and to experience it—the
demands on the self that being a king involves.

73

VI

Hamlet and Our Problems

HENRY V, by virtue of his public role, is forced to be something of an actor—hence his apprenticeship at roleplaying in *Henry IV*. But every private man is an actor too—for our acts are often performances, in the sense that they strive either to express or conceal something that we think of as inside us, our true self. We are all actors, then, to a degree. But in the ordinary, professional sense of the word, what is an actor? An actor is a man who wants to play Hamlet. Playing the role of the Prince proves you are truly an actor and not a clown, an entertainer, a personality, a "type," or a movie star. It is the ultimate validation of an actor's professional status—and yet, curiously enough, it is far from being the hardest of acting tasks. Most men of the theater would probably accept Sir John Gielgud's characterization of the play as "audience-proof"; and certainly Macready's observation remains true today: a total failure in the role is rare.[1] Many other parts are harder to make a success of, and some—like King Lear —demand skills which the successful actor of Hamlet may not possess. But Hamlet strikes us as somehow unique in requiring and displaying the actor's art.

Why should this be so? One answer lies in the variety that Dr. Johnson recognized as a distinguishing excellence of the play. No other role offers so much action of so many different kinds. Hamlet is soldier, scholar, statesman, madman, fencer, critic, magnani-

[1] Rosamond Gilder, *John Gielgud's Hamlet* (New York, 1937), p. 50; *Macready's Reminiscences and Selections from His Diaries and Letters*, ed. Sir Frederick Pollock (New York, 1875), p. 37.

mous prince, cunning revenger, aloof noble, witty iron-
ist, man of the people, etc.; and he is regularly required
to change from one role to another before our eyes or
to maintain several—or a disarming mixture of several
—at once. The play abounds in situations that require
the principal actor to shift his mood or mode of action
because of a change in audience. A number of examples result from Hamlet's having to deceive those
around him, but there are many occasions when the
shift does not come about as a result of the necessity
for self-protection ("Horatio, or I do forget myself,"
the jokes with the gravedigger, his toying with Osric,
the address to the players, the grand apology to Laertes). And there are intermediate stages where we cannot say with any precision whether Hamlet is "acting"
or not. These are all occasions on which we are keenly
aware of the actor's range and of the pleasures it can
give us, of the different things the man on the stage
is able to do and do well, and of his skill in making
something coherent out of this variety.

The problems involved here are in an important
sense exemplary of all acting. For as Hamlet suggests
in his speech to the players, there is a critical technical
and aesthetic difficulty inherent in the variety available
to any professional actor. Great acting demands "tem-
perance," "smoothness," moderation, control—and variety tests this control to the full. Lear is required to
do just one kind of thing for most of his play, a very
momentous and demanding kind of thing to be sure,
but his problem as an actor is to find sufficient variety
(and reserves of energy) to get through the evening.
Hamlet's problem, assuming he is competent to execute
the incredibly many separate "bits" the play allows him,
is to control them, to focus them, to find an overall
conception in which each has its place, and to give a
meaningful smoothness to his transitions. Hamlet is
not urging any principle of simple realism when he re-

minds the actors that their art consists in holding the mirror up to nature. The actor's task is to interpret life:

to show virtue her own feature, scorn her own image, and the very age and body of the time his form and pressure. (III, ii, 25-27)

It is Prince Hamlet's task, too, and his problems are very similar to those of the actor who plays him.

Hamlet awakes in its audience a unique concern for the actor's art—and particularly for his interpretive skill, his ability to make satisfying sense out of all the actions he is called upon to perform. It is possible to ask of an actor who portrays King Lear, "How will he get through it?" and the "it"—what Lear undergoes—will be on our minds as much as Lear himself. But with Hamlet we ask as of no other play, "How will he act the part?"

We do not ask, "Will he make any sense of it?" In the theater at least *Hamlet* runs no risk of obscurity. Indeed one of the problems of Hamlet, and one reason why the role is both a supreme challenge and one in which it is very hard to fail utterly, is that even a crude, simplifying, singleminded interpretation—a making one kind of sense but not full sense of the role—can produce solid, effective theater.

Interpretation is one of the necessary questions of *Hamlet*; to an important extent it is something the play is "about." Like its chief character, *Hamlet* draws our attention to varieties of action and to the questions of interpretation they raise. Our experience of *Hamlet* in the theater is primarily an attempt to follow an action so various, intricate, and proliferating that it cries out for interpretation at every turn. The "problems" of the play point, finally, to the subtle means it employs for manipulating one of our most fundamental theatrical appetites: the desire for action that makes sense, especially for action that seems complete and resolved.

As an example, consider III, iii, where Hamlet comes upon the King at prayer. What does the audience see? Two great antagonists who have been maneuvering toward each other throughout the play are alone together at last. They do not look at each other. They do not act. In fact each is frozen in a posture that manifestly suggests an action he does not perform. We see a praying man and his armed opponent. Hamlet has brought his father's murderer to his knees. But the praying man is not praying and the man with the sword is not going to strike. The King, however, wants to pray, just as Hamlet wants to kill the King. The moment we have waited for so patiently arrives and it is not what we meant at all. It is a scene of extraordinary and peculiar tension. The frozen action allows us to register simultaneously an intense impulse to action, an incompleted action, and no action—action whose meaning may be the opposite of what we see. Criticism of this scene has focused on the reasons Hamlet gives for not killing Claudius, but clearly any doubts we may have as to the significance of what Hamlet says at this point are only part of our response to this powerfully engaging stage image, only one of many uncertainties as to action and its interpretation that are being deployed in us. But "doubt" and "uncertainty" tend to suggest speculative states, reflective categories that might be applied to the play in retrospect. Though they are not inaccurate to describe part of our feeling in the theater, they obscure the major source of that feeling and hence its precise quality, which springs from the maneuvering of bodies on the stage and the rhythm of our response to the action as it unfolds.

To understand this more fully, an important technical device must be discussed. III, iii is one of a number of places in *Hamlet*—particularly toward the middle of the play—where what might be called a "stop-action" technique is used, that is, where one or more players is stopped in mid-gesture and the action frozen in a variety of ways. As, for instance, when the First Player describes Pyrrhus stopping in the very act of killing Priam:

> for, lo! his sword,
> Which was declining on the milky head
> Of reverend Priam, seem'd i' th' air to stick.
> So, as a painted tyrant, Pyrrhus stood
> And, like a neutral to his will and matter,
> Did nothing.   (ii, ii, 499-504)

It helps to visualize the Player performing in a style which marks him off as an "actor" from the other figures on stage, gesturing overemphatically, throwing himself into the part ("Look whe'er he has not turn'd his colour and has tears in's eyes"). We may expect that the player has suited the action to the word and frozen grandly.

The Player continues. Pyrrhus's gesture is started up again, but only after preparatory verbal fanfare that again draws attention to the stopped action:

> But, as we often see, against some storm,
> A silence in the heavens, the rack stand still,
> The bold winds speechless, and the orb below
> As hush as death, anon the dreadful thunder
> Doth rend the region; so, after Pyrrhus' pause,
> Aroused vengeance sets him new a-work;
> And never did the Cyclops' hammers fall
> On Mars his armour forg'd for proof eterne
> With less remorse than Pyrrhus' bleeding sword
> Now falls on Priam.   (505-14)

A few lines later Polonius stops him; he starts up once again, and immediately Hamlet interrupts! (It might be noted that Hamlet in giving the first few lines of the speech interrupts himself twice. The pattern of interruption contributes to the stop-action configuration, though there is probably little gesture or physical action to interrupt.)

Hamlet's soliloquy after the players leave turns on a violent self-interruption, as the Prince catches himself in the full flight of some great melodramatic gesture:

. . . Bloody, bawdy villain!
Remorseless, treacherous, lecherous, kindless villain!
O, vengeance!
Why, what an ass am I . . .   (608-11)

Again the shortened line ("O, vengeance!") orchestrates a stopped action.[2] Here, as at so many points in the play, we are made conscious of the fine line between genuine intensity and pose. Indeed, there is no line—and this is what the stop-action reveals. Hamlet's response is genuine in the sense that it is strongly felt, irresistible, and grows naturally and persuasively out of the situation. There is nothing in the preparation that suggests pretense, nor need there be. Hamlet is throwing himself into the role of revenger. But by interrupting himself at the height of his outburst, by freezing the pose, Hamlet draws our attention to his theatricality of gesture and language. At this moment, sincerity and "acting" are hard to tell apart—and one is not necessarily to be preferred to the other. In fact, Hamlet now is prompted by revulsion at his own playacting to use a much more elaborate piece of theatricality to catch the conscience of the King—the play within the play. The sudden break has allowed action to be revealed as acting, and has also involved us more

[2] The authenticity of this line has been questioned. But if Harold Jenkins is right, and it represents a playhouse interpolation, it still casts light on the way the speech was performed, and very likely on its intended effect. The actor felt the need or opportunity for marking the punctuation, for heightening the frozen posture with a posturing phrase. In any case, the stop-action is plain even without "O vengeance!" (See "Playhouse Interpolations in the Folio Text of *Hamlet*," *Studies in Bibliography*, XIII [1960], 31-47.)

79

deeply in doubt as to the ultimate direction or interpretation of any action.[3]

The stop-action tableaus play upon a question that recurs in various forms throughout *Hamlet*: when is an action not an action? It is raised of course in the "To be or not to be" soliloquy, where Hamlet—who has a moment ago appeared ready to catch the conscience of the King—now analyzes the conditions under which action loses its name or falls into non-being. Hamlet sees his situation as paradoxical—action results in not being. To be is not to act. And the question *when is an action not an action?* reappears in a dozen guises, as, for example, when is revenge not revenge? when is a madman not a madman? when is a mother not a mother? when is a funeral not a funeral? when is a suicide not a suicide? when is play in earnest?[4] If there is a "question of Hamlet" it is this. As the role of Hamlet itself directs our attention to the problems of interpreting and making sense out of action, so the play is endlessly varying the motif of doubt as to the significance of action.

[3] Two or three other moments of stop-action deserve mention. The action of the play scene itself is stopped in a number of ways. The dumb show allows us to preview the murder of Gonzago in the slow-motion of pantomime, and later the performance is broken off sharply before the climax. The entrance of the Ghost in III, iv provides yet another example. Hamlet breaks off in the midst of his attack on the Queen to bend his eye on vacancy, and they are fixed in this tableau for several lines.

Robert Hapgood discusses a number of "arrested actions" in his "Hamlet Nearly Absurd: The Dramaturgy of Delay," *Tulane Drama Review* (Summer, 1965), pp. 132-45; several of his examples strike me as contributing to the effects described above. I should add, however, that Hapgood's understanding of these moments (which he treats primarily as instances of delay) seems to be very different from mine.

[4] Cf. Maynard Mack's superb essay, "The World of *Hamlet*," *Yale Review*, 41 (1952), 513-14. My concern is less with the authenticity of "acts," as Professor Mack's is, than with the problems posed by our appetite for significant "action."

The famous problem of whether Hamlet is active or inactive may be understood as a misleading abstraction from this type of effect. The Prince may be described as either active or inactive because in *Hamlet* action is constantly losing its name. Though there is an endless variety of it, we are always aware—as in the stop-action sequences—of our appetite for a certain kind of completeness, a meaningfulness which we as members of the audience demand of action.

The critical approach that focuses on Hamlet's "inaction" typically concerns itself with his speculative capacities. But the familiar distinction that this interpretation turns on—between action and reason—is inappropriate to the play. Hamlet's Renaissance sense of human dignity unites reason and action in a single continuum. Man is a great piece of work because his capacity for both reason and action, for reason in action, is divine. Not only does reason exist to prompt us to action, it is only *used* when we act:

> Sure, He that made us with such large discourse,
> Looking before and after, gave us not
> That capability and god-like reason
> To fust in us unus'd.   (IV, iv, 36-39)

The actions that matter, of course, are the ones that make satisfying sense—full sense, not like Laertes' half-cocked rebellion, say, but like Hamlet's ultimate revenge. The importance of reason in action in *Hamlet*, of action that is meaningful in the face of difficult situations, may be seen if we compare three familiar speeches from the beginning, middle, and end of the play. The "To be or not to be" soliloquy where significant action is inhibited by the fear of death, is a paradoxical reversal of Hamlet's first soliloquy, in which he longs for death because he can no longer attribute significance to action ("How weary, stale, flat, and unprofitable,/ Seems to me all the uses of this world"). But by the end of the play he sees a unifying meaning to all his actions; his life is now a "story" ("And in this harsh world draw thy breath in pain/ To tell my story"). He is only afraid that death will keep it from being apparent to others.

Reason and action are not opposed in *Hamlet*, but for most of the play they fail to coalesce as either we or the characters would like them to. Without intelligible meaning, action is unsatisfying or disturbing, a fact exploited from the opening scene. We feel there not only doubt and interrogation but an immediate pressure to sort out the significances of a peculiarly tense and busy action. (Who's on duty here? Why does the wrong guard challenge? Why are they trying to get rid of Francisco? What does the ghost mean? Why are they on guard?) Our response is natural, as is that of the characters. Action and reason seek their meaning in each other, and nowhere more than in *Hamlet*. This may help to account for the special emphasis the play gives to the theme of speech (e.g. its concern with the way actors speak, the significant use of the word "discourse," the prominence of Osric, Hamlet's emphatic "say" at II, ii, 596, where one would ordinarily expect "do")—for speech is a kind of intermediary step between willing significance and establishing it. It is neither reason nor action, but a reaching out of one toward the other. And it is exactly this effort that the action of *Hamlet* repeatedly highlights and foils.

Most of the characters are engaged in a continuing struggle to find out—and interpret—what the others are doing or have done. Their efforts may be said to come to a head when Hamlet confronts the Queen. His address to the players has contained hints of the stress he will be under in this scene. In the very torrent, tempest, and whirlwind of his passion he will have to be careful, as the Ghost has warned him, not to o'erstep the modesty of nature. It is his toughest acting assignment so far, and when he comes to it he quite literally sets out to hold a mirror up to nature:

Come, come, and sit you down. You shall not
    budge.
You go not till I set you up a glass
Where you may see the inmost part of you.
                (III, iv, 18-20)

Again the difficult relations between action, acting, and
the self come to the fore. Gertrude is a striking example
of divorce between action and meaning. She has allowed herself to sleep with Claudius and become his
queen largely by refusing to think about what she has
been doing. She has followed her senses and blocked
out the meaning of her actions. "What have I done?"
is her revealing cry, and Hamlet proceeds to interpret
for her (the italics are, of course, mine):

> HAMLET
> Such an *act*
> That blurs the grace and blush of modesty
> . . . O, such a *deed*
> As from the body of contraction plucks
> The very soul . . .
> Yea, this solidity and compound mass,
> With tristful visage, as against the doom,
> Is thought-sick at the *act*.
> QUEEN
> Ay me, what *act*,
> That roars so loud and thunders in the index?
>   (40-52)

The fierce and disturbing intensity of their dialogue
derives from Hamlet's insistence on the physical actu-
ality of his mother's crime. He wants to make her *see*,
to put action and meaning together, just as he has
wanted to say what is in his heart and to act on his cue
for revenge. But at the very moment Hamlet is trying
to make the Queen interpret her own actions, a great
tangle of misinterpretation forms around them. Polo-

nius thinks Hamlet will kill the Queen. Hamlet thinks Polonius is the King. On two separate occasions and for different reasons, Gertrude thinks Hamlet is mad. To these we may add the Queen's "What have I done?" and our own curiosity as to why she doesn't see the Ghost. As so often in the play, an increasing pressure toward clarity has carried us into deeper uncertainty and doubt.

To act significantly in these circumstances it is necessary to be an actor—to play a part and hence to use disguise, to be and not to be. One's inmost part may be that which passeth show, and any action may be such as a man might play, but some kind of playacting seems necessary to reveal what ordinary action keeps hidden. After the play-within-the-play Hamlet has announced, in rhetoric that reminds us of the theatricality of the revenger's occupation ("'Tis now the very witching time of night . . . Now could I drink hot blood") that he is ready for violent action—but with his mother he intends only to act the part, "I will speak daggers to her, but use none." Though his appearance will perfectly suit the reality within him, it will be only a pretense. He will act and not act, but the acting will be so effective that it will cause Polonius to cry out from behind the arras and result in a violence Hamlet did not (and did) intend. Hamlet has now been seen twice to attack the King and not to attack him, and he concludes the scene with his mother by saying goodnight five times before he leaves.

The play, then, is full of action, but the action is handled in such a way that our responses perform in effect an analysis of the feelings and appetites we attach to the very notion of action. We are regularly invited to complete an action—to consider what it means, to anticipate where it may lead—only to have our response blocked, distracted, or diverted, compromised in some way. The stop-action sequences; the early air of mystery; the multiple networks of doubt, deceit, and detection; the stress given to nuances and paradoxes of acting technique; the teasing verbal play with reason and action, saying and doing, being and not being, all contribute to this effect.[5]

Considered in this light, many matters which have

[5] There are a number of attractive minor examples of action losing its name. When the Ghost speaks up from the cellarage and Hamlet calls upon his friends to swear secrecy, the same action is repeated three or four times to the accompaniment of the Ghost's "Swear . . . Swear . . . Swear by his sword . . . Swear" [following Q_2]. The repetition tends to leach the solemnity out of the action, to blur its clarity in the very act of insisting on it—to detach the significant gesture from the felt significance.

Similarly, when Horatio brings his great news to Hamlet in the first act, they are so incapable of interpreting each other correctly they are forced to repeat themselves:

HAMLET
My father!—methinks I see my father.
HORATIO
Oh, where, my lord?
HAMLET
In my mind's eye, Horatio. . . .
HORATIO
My lord, I think I saw him yesternight.
HAMLET
Saw? Who?
HORATIO
My lord, the King your father.
HAMLET
The King my father!

(ii, 184-91)

Actions are frequently repeated, allowing us to note the effect of different interpretations. Hamlet and the First Player recite the same speech; Claudius's treason is narrated by the Ghost, acted in dumb show and then again with words. Osric plays the fop and Hamlet imitates him. And there is a very funny and intricate variation on the theme of sincerity when Hamlet insists on welcoming Rosencrantz and Guildenstern *a second time* before welcoming the players. He insists that he must overact this second reception, so that when he acts less sincerely (he claims) for the players it will not falsify the meaning of his welcome to his old school friends:

provoked critical disagreement in the past may be recognized not as problems requiring solutions one way or the other, but as signs of the play's careful management of our response. The first act, for example, ends with Hamlet vowing vengeance and promising some secret course of action toward that end. In II, i, we learn that Hamlet has appeared to Ophelia in marvellous disarray, apparently mad. Is this part of his plan? The answer is that there are simply too many variables for us to be certain. When the Bristol Old Vic presented the play in New York, Hamlet actually appeared in this scene—out of Polonius's line of vision—and with a number of broad winks conveyed to Ophelia —and us—that he was just kidding; it was all part of the antic disposition. This is one way of clearing up the action, but it is not Shakespeare's way, which is not to clear it up. It is Hamlet's absence from the stage that gives the scene its significance. Shakespeare might have introduced him, could have rearranged existing material to do so. But without Hamlet we are forced to guess whether his charade was deliberately intended to mislead, or an expression of the anguish that is also developed in Act I. We only know for sure that Polonius's interpretation is wrong.

Shakespeare could also easily have allowed Hamlet to resolve another problem that has perplexed the critics: whether any significant delay occurs between

---

GUILDENSTERN
There are the players.
HAMLET
Gentlemen, you are welcome to Elsinore. Your hands, come. The appurtenance of welcome is fashion and ceremony. Let me comply with you in the garb, lest my extent to the players, which, I tell you, must show fairly outward, should more appear like entertainment than yours. You are welcome.

(II, ii, 386-93)

He probably repeats his gestures of welcome two or three times during the speech.

Acts I and II. This is not simply a matter of the flexible time dimension of the Elizabethan stage. Shakespeare can be very explicit about linear time when it suits him. He can also deliberately follow an impossible sequence, as in *Othello*, and keep us from noticing—and he can simply be careless of time when it doesn't matter. But he does none of these things in this case. He does finally let us know that Hamlet has spent more time than he would have liked between I, v and II, i, but he allows us this information only at the very end of Act II. Thus, here—and elsewhere—the question of whether Hamlet delays unnecessarily is deliberately left opaque. There are good reasons for him to delay, but they are fed to us at the wrong time dramatically and in the wrong way for us to be confident that they are the right ones, or even to be sure the delay has been so egregious as at moments he claims it is.[6] The play of course does not permit us to fall into careful examination of these questions; they exist only as part of the pattern of interrupted action and blocked significance.

The pattern (like the Oedipal pattern) is designed to excite both our deepest interest and our deepest resistance. Unfortunately, because it is so original (and perhaps because it is disturbing) it has often provoked stupid "improvements." Since the "To be or not to be" soliloquy breaks the arc of feeling between Hamlet's appearance in II, ii and III, ii, many companies follow the mutilated First Quarto and place it in the midst of II, ii. It makes more "sense" that way, that is, it makes it easier to interpret Hamlet. For similar reasons, III, iii, which unexpectedly detours Hamlet into the King's

[6] "How all occasions do inform against me" (IV, iv, 32ff) gives us our strongest sense that Hamlet delays, and is the source for most critical speculation as to his reasons. But it should be observed that the soliloquy occurs at the only point in the play where Hamlet, under guard and on his way to England, has absolutely no opportunity for revenge.

closet, was for more than two centuries either omitted or substantially cut in most performances. But in both cases the break in our expectations, the resistance to interpretation, is vital.

Critics concerned with the problem of Hamlet's delay have long concentrated on the scene with Claudius and with reason. But the question to be asked here is not why does Hamlet delay, but why does the play delay—why are *we* delayed? There is more than a grain of truth in the facetious statement that Hamlet delays because there would be no play if he did not. Part of our response to the closet scene depends on our knowledge that the play cannot end here—and not merely because we have paid for an hour's more entertainment. As soon as Hamlet enters we know he will not kill the King. He cannot kill Claudius at prayer, not for theological reasons, sound as they may be, but for aesthetic ones. It is undramatic, too easy. The King's back is to him. There is no source of resistance. The play is going elsewhere. The action, we realize, would not satisfy us, though like Hamlet we have longed for it since the first act. If Shakespeare ever played with an audience, it is here: once again our desire for significant action is drawn upon in a way that also arouses our latent sense of how difficult this appetite is to satisfy.

When two such deeply opposed antagonists have been kept apart for so long by actions of such brilliance and complexity, we come to need an ending that will release all our pent-up energies. We need a spacious ending, a great clarifying release. And this is what we get in the splendid free-for-all that concludes the play, in which the King is hoist on both his petards, and Hamlet, after a display of athletic, military, and moral virtuosity, kills him in full possession of palpably damning evidence and is vindicated before a large audience. To the characters on stage the scene is confusion,

88

an example of the futility of all efforts to force a significance on action, to grasp what Hamlet calls the invisible event. It is a tableau, finally, of "purposes mistook/ Fall'n on the inventors' heads," but for us it is nothing of the sort. If an Elizabethan audience wanted to refer it to a theological principle they might see it as an example of the workings of Providence, but their rhythm of response to the action would be much the same as ours. All through the play we have been reminded, both explicitly and by the imagery and movement of the verse, of the pleasure that attends any great release of energy in ample and unambiguous action:

> ... in grace whereof,
> No jocund health that Denmark drinks to-day,
> But the great cannon to the clouds shall tell,
> And the King's rouse the heavens shall bruit again,
> Re-speaking earthly thunder.　　(I, ii, 124-28)

> But I will delve one yard below their mines,
> And blow them at the moon. O, 'tis most sweet,
> When in one line two crafts directly meet.
> 　　　　　　　　　　　(III, iv, 208-210)

> And let the kettle to the trumpets speak,
> The trumpet to the cannoneer without,
> The cannons to the heavens, the heaven to earth.
> 　　　　　　　　　　　(V, ii, 286-88)

Even when Claudius uses the opposite figure of a missile missing its target, he does it by way of another beautiful evocation of a sudden, sweeping, clearly aimed discharge

> Whose whisper o'er the world's diameter,
> As level as the cannon to his blank,
> Transports his poisoned shot, may miss our name,
> And hit the woundless air.　　(IV, i, 41-44)

Now the final release comes in a scene which rarely fails to produce an overwhelming excitement and satisfaction.

Pressure toward a full physical clash onstage has begun at least as early as Hamlet's failure to kill the King at prayer, and progressed through his taunting of the King and escaping his guards, Laertes' abortive attack on Claudius, and Hamlet's inconclusive struggle with Laertes in the grave. We are also given the details of a wonderful fight at sea and the just deserts of Rosencrantz and Guildenstern (which is also the result of "a kind of fighting"). At last Hamlet is asked to "play" with Laertes, and the fencing match begins. It is an action whose significance keeps shifting: it means different things at different moments for the different players. And simultaneously we are aware of the gratifying opportunities it offers the actors. The court ceremony is elaborate. The fencing must be excellent. Nowhere is the Prince more various. The actors must show the difference between fencing in play and fighting in deadly earnest, with at least one intermediary stage between. But if the bystanders on the stage are confused by the results, we for once are not. All the significances are clear and we watch them explode into action. Every piece of inner villainy leaves its telltale outer mark and is repaid in fully emblematic action. ("The point envenom'd too!/ Then, venom, to thy work!") The purpose of playing is achieved; acting and being are one. In form and moving all is express and admirable.

The play ends with a final unambiguous discharge of energy. Fortinbras, who has a soldier's simple sense of what is appropriate, orders a peal of ordnance shot off. The air has been cleared. We have experienced, in this long heightening and ultimate fulfillment of our basic theatrical desires, the equivalent of Hamlet's tangled meditations on action and human worth. Hamlet has been concerned from the first with the good actor's root problem—sincerity. Any gesture is, after all, such as a man might play, but if this is the case how does one truthfully perform what is within him? In an earlier chapter I pointed out that Hamlet seems to be about eighteen at the play's beginning and thirty near its end. As a factual question the problem is of little importance, and there is nothing that absolutely contradicts the specific figure of thirty given by the gravedigger. But it is interesting that the two ages often mark a great change in a man's understanding of sincerity. At eighteen the imperative is not to live a lie. By thirty, one realizes how hard it is to be certain one isn't.

The problem of sincerity is of interest only in those for whom it is difficult. The obvious sincerity of Fortinbras, Laertes, and the First Player leave Hamlet irritated or envious. There is nothing within them that passes show. But to say "I have that within which passeth show," is really to challenge the whole enterprise of theater; it is to say I have a self which cannot be sounded in action, that any encounter I have with the world must merely be playacting in a derogatory sense. The crisis of young Hamlet's life comes when he is forced to act, forced by the Ghost to find a show that will be true to what is within him and to the world in which he finds himself. As with the actor who plays the role, the greatest strain falls on Hamlet's capacity for expressive coherence, for action that at each moment is true to the delicacy and difficulty of his entire situation. The tragic effect comes because we are made to feel that this achievement is possible for Hamlet only at the cost of great destruction.

A good way to see the nature of Prince Hamlet's difficulty in its relation to tragic emotion is to contrast his play with *Julius Caesar*, the tragedy immediately preceding it in composition. Prince Hamlet strikes us as an intellectual for much the same reasons Brutus does; we see them deliberating certain problems of action and attempting to formulate them in abstract terms. But Brutus's problem is that he would like to separate significance from the agents that produce significance. Though he cannot kill Caesar's spirit without killing Caesar, he tries to limit the significance of his act to the spiritual, to treat the "genius" as if it were independent of its "mortal instruments." Hamlet's problem, on the other hand, is to *attach* significance to action, to overcome his initial sense that all the uses of the world are flat and unprofitable, to fully unite action and reason, to find a revenge which is both internally and externally satisfying, an action that like all good acting holds the mirror up to nature.

But the achievement of clarity and full expressiveness in action is immensely difficult for Hamlet and immensely expensive. The destructive or demonic force that we are accustomed to encounter in tragedy seems in *Julius Caesar* to rise from the body of Caesar itself and is exemplified first in the blood that floods the stage and later in Caesar's ghost. The source of the energy that destroys Brutus, then, is the very element of the problem he has tried to overcome—Caesar's inescapable physicality, the mortal instruments that become genius only by virtue of their mortality. In the same way, Hamlet is finally destroyed and fulfilled by an action whose source is beyond his control. It is only when he has agreed not to force a significance upon his actions, not to look before and after but to let be, that he is swept to his revenge. The revenge kills him as it has also killed Gertrude, Ophelia, and Polonius. The destructive element turns out to be the very element in his situation which he has struggled in his mind to root out and overcome—whatever there is in the self that the mind cannot grasp and control in thought and adequately express in action.

We are thus brought back to the dubieties of the great central soliloquy. There are more things in heaven and earth than any man's philosophy can unravel. A taint of death lies not only in every action but in discourse of reason itself. Being and not being, play-acting and sincerity, action and letting be, the pressure to clarity and the proliferation of doubt are inextricably intertwined in mortal experience. Shakespeare's tragic heroes are men who insist on the self-destruction proper to their genius; sooner or later they seek out that death which allows their capacities most fully to illuminate the world for the audience that watches them die. The destruction Hamlet seeks allows him to take as far as possible and to test to the full an impulse we all to some extent share, and to which the art of the theater is dedicated—through action to make sense of life.

VII

The Worst of
King Lear

At the end of IV, i of *King Lear*, Gloucester directs Edgar to take him to Dover. His words, like so many in the play, seem to have a wide and rich application to its entire action:

> There is a cliff, whose high and bending head
> Looks fearfully in the confined deep.
> Bring me but to the very brim of it,
> And I'll repair the misery thou dost bear
> With something rich about me.   (76-80)

Taken by themselves, these lines constitute a little poem on the nature of tragedy. Like Lear, in whom Nature stands on the verge of her confine, Gloucester is made to see (in spite of his blindness) deep into the fearful abyss ("How fearful/ And dizzy 'tis, to cast one's eyes so low"). We do not accompany Lear beyond the edge. (We cannot, for example, tell what his last glimpse of Cordelia's lips has shown him.) Indeed we are frequently made to feel how hard it is to follow him as far as we do, but we sense that by accompanying him, with effort, in his trip to the brink, we are given "something rich about him" that is somehow related to the misery we bear.

Of course the misery we bear most immediately in the play is the pain of watching it, and the punishing aspect of the play—the indignities, tortures, and violations the actors' bodies suffer, and through them our own—cannot be overemphasized in our reading of the play or even, I believe, in production; at any rate, they are easily underemphasized.

94

The history of *Lear* in the theater has been a continuing search for new ways to make the play easier for actors and audience to take. To an extent this is a part of its design. Even those productions that mean to "bring *Lear* home" to the audience seem always to involve fresh bluntings and blurrings of the full effect. Peter Brook's mounting of the play, for example, was heavily indebted to Jan Kott, the author of *Shakespeare Our Contemporary* and a critic particularly alert—often with valuable results—to violence and "cruelty" in Shakespeare. But the production scarcely came to grips with the play's full unpleasantness. The idea was to emphasize that Shakespeare is as contemporary as Samuel Beckett, which is a little like emphasizing that Mozart is as contemporary as Satie. The suffering of *King Lear* was planed down to affectlessness;[1] and though this passed as a very immediate and close-to-the-bone version of the play, the reason it was so acceptable is that it was—compared to the full *King Lear*— so painless. Brook's interpretation had the great virtue of being manageable; it was under control as productions of *Lear* seldom are. It succeeded in giving us the impression of going through a great deal of horror

[1] For accounts of Brook's production (pro and con) that reinforce this impression, see Charles Marowitz, "Lear Log," *Tulane Drama Review* (Winter, 1963), pp. 103-121; and Robert Speaight, "Shakespeare in Britain," *Shakespeare Quarterly*, XIV (1963), 419-21. The exact sense of affectlessness conveyed may have resulted not simply from Brook's approach but from its interaction with the peculiar strengths and weaknesses of Scofield's performance. (See Marowitz, pp. 118-19.) Interestingly, Scofield seems not to have felt particularly influenced by the analogy with Beckett, indeed to have considered it limiting. (See Carol Carlisle, *Shakespeare from the Greenroom: Actors' Criticisms of Four Major Tragedies* [Chapel Hill, 1969], p. 291.)

Though I differ with Peter Brook over *King Lear*, I would be sorry to leave the impression that I have anything but the highest regard for him as a director of Shakespeare. He is a remarkable artist, and shows us more of Shakespeare's meaning when he is wrong about it than most of us do when we are right.

without having to digest it. Paul Scofield was able to emerge from his performance relatively unscathed. (I say "relatively" since Scofield makes a specialty of looking scathed; he seemed no more so at the end than at the beginning.) Now, affectlessness is a revealing mood and it has its place in *King Lear*, especially toward the end when the more ordinary characters begin to cave in before the spectacle of Lear's suffering. *Endgame*, which according to Kott and Brook is the play's modern analogue, makes unrelieved affectlessness illuminating by turning it into elegant and varied, if black comedy. But this is not the method of Shakespeare's play.

It is perhaps only natural to look at *King Lear* and decide that since it contains so much horror its dominant mood must be beaten numbness and monotony. Certainly the response tells us something true about the play. There is more pain in it than we easily know what to do with. In an age of the knowledge of extreme pain, which is for most of us knowledge of the extreme pain of others, it is comforting to believe that affectlessness is the worst pain. It allows us to think that our sympathies are really adequate to our full experience while at the same time saving us from total disintegration in the face of the daily paper and the T.V. news. Gifted comedians like Beckett may probe our affectlessness by brilliant imitations of monotony, but the danger is that we are all too ready to believe that monotony itself is the deepest truth pain knows. Monotony may be the final condition of the suffering body and as such a blessed release, but it is not the worst suffering nor the truth of suffering. The victims of torture may be allowed the escape into affectlessness, if they can find it—but not artists or their audiences.

King Lear is designed to confront torture, not numbness. It is also deeply aware of our desire to escape. Take for example simply what we see in the scene already referred to, the physical atrocity of the tableau of

Gloucester and Edgar. Gloucester is not only recently blinded, humiliated, and suicidal—his eyes are bleeding. Edgar too is a horrible sight, a fact easily overlooked in reading and largely missed in productions, where he is usually a well set-up *jeune premier* in a blanket. His father tells us that when he first saw him on the heath he "made me think a man a worm," and Edgar has explained in some detail exactly how he proposes to transform himself:

> I will preserve myself, and am bethought
> To take the basest and most poorest shape
> That ever penury, in contempt of man,
> Brought near to beast. My face I'll grime
>   with filth,
> Blanket my loins, elf all my hairs in knots,
> And with presented nakedness out-face
> The winds and persecutions of the sky.
> The country gives me proof and precedent
> Of Bedlam beggars, who, with roaring voices,
> Strike in their numb'd and mortified bare arms
> Pins, wooden pricks, nails, sprigs of rosemary;
> And with this horrible object, from low farms,
> Poor pelting villages, sheep-cotes, and mills,
> Sometimes with lunatic bans, sometimes with
>   prayers,
> Enforce their charity.[2]   (II, iii, 6-20)

There is no reason not to take him at his word. On the stage Edgar must be filthy, grotesque, very nearly naked, and bear on his body evidence of horrible mutilation. He is the kind of beggar who *enforces* charity—so repellent, nasty, and noisy that you pay him to go away. We have all seen beggars of this type, though they are infrequent in American cities because the mode is not profitable. Edgar is not the ingratiating panhandler, or the collapsed wino, or the pitiable or-

[2] I follow the Quarto reading for "bare" in l. 15; Folio omits.

phan of the storm, and certainly not the decent young man down on his luck that actors frequently portray him to be. He is the kind that sticks his stump in your face. He does not set out to inspire feelings of benevolence, pity, or human solidarity. We give to him because we cannot stand him, because his body is a fearful reminder of the deformity that life may visit upon us at any instant.

Why, then, do we so seldom find Edgar played this way? One important reason is that it would make things very hard for the actor who has to play Lear. Edgar is usually presented as a kind of masquerade-party madman so as to contrast with Lear's genuine madness. The contrast of course is just the point, but Edgar's masquerade is a horrible and *convincing* affair; his life depends on it. The primary effect of the contrast is not to show up the artifice of Edgar's madness but to drive home the intensity of Lear's. Unfortunately the actor playing the King still has ahead of him the Dover scenes, the adultery speech, and the death of Cordelia; his problem is how to endure his part. Full loathsomeness for Edgar means added impossibilities for Lear. And this technical problem reflects our larger experience of the play. We say of Lear, "How can he go on? How much more is he—are we—to suffer?" Just as the characters in *Hamlet* keep asking questions about the meaning of action, the characters in *King Lear* keep inquiring about suffering: how much more there is to endure and what they are to conclude from it.

The audience quickly recognizes how cautious it must be about resolving on the "meaning of suffering" in *King Lear*—or at least about finding a single meaning —because it is a subject on which so many pronouncements are made in the play, only to be undercut by the continuing action. When Albany learns that Cornwall is dead he cries, "This shows you are above,/ You justicers," and one of our impulses is to agree. But it is scarcely five minutes since we have had to sit through the excruciating scene of Gloucester's blinding, and in the interim Gloucester has appeared once more, with bleeding eyes. Whatever our convictions as to justice and divinity, be they Elizabethan or existentialist, our immediate response is to add another, conflicting feeling to the one we share with Albany. And Albany's mind follows the same oscillation—a characteristic one in the play—from summing up the meaning of sorrow to feeling it anew:

> This shows you are above,
> You justicers, that these our nether crimes
> So speedily can venge! But, O poor Gloucester!
>
> (IV, ii, 78-80)

It is no wonder that two of the most familiar quotations from *King Lear* cancel each other out:

> As flies to wanton boys, are we to th' gods,
> They kill us for their sport. (IV, i, 38-39)

> The gods are just, and of our pleasant vices,
> Make instruments to plague us.
>
> (V, iii, 170-71)

Edgar in particular has a gift for confidently formulating some principle about the uses, limits, or significance of suffering only to have it shattered by succeeding events. At the end of III, vi he has said:

> When we our betters see bearing our woes,
> We scarcely think our miseries our foes.
> . . . But then the mind much sufferance doth o'erskip,
> When grief hath mates, and bearing fellowship.
> How light and portable my pain seems now.
>
> (109-115)

But his next scene will show the fallacy of this comforting reflection; Edgar's grief will only be increased by the "fellowship" of his father. In IV, i he establishes another familiar principle—when things are at the

worst they can only get better—which again he quickly
has to abandon. ("The worst is not/ So long as we can
say 'This is the worst.' ")

Gloucester shares the family weakness for half-baked
moral observations. In the same scene he says to Poor
Tom:

Here, take this purse, thou whom the heavens' plagues
Have humbled to all strokes. That I am wretched
Makes thee the happier.   (67-69)

Gloucester is wrong on both counts. Edgar is *not* inured
to all strokes, and there is no closed economy of misery: Gloucester's purse does not make him happier.

This constant return to the theme of what is the
worst and to the uses of suffering is of course part of
the large pattern of accumulation and reduction which
has often been noted in the play. In *Hamlet* the characteristic of the action is variety—new stimuli, changes of
direction, pirates, players, ghosts, Hamlet as courtier,
Hamlet as punster, Hamlet as bitter satirist, Hamlet as
near-suicide, Hamlet as cunning revenger, etc. Appropriately in the language of *Hamlet* the tendency is toward groups of words that distinguish, vary, multiply
distinctions ("dead waste and middle of the night,"
"tempest, torrent and whirlwind of your passion," "to
show the very age and body of the time his form and
pressure"). In *King Lear* on the other hand the characteristic of the action is *more of the same*, rejection
by one daughter and then another, the putting out of
one eye and then the other. We go not simply from bad
to worse, but from worst to worse. Likewise, in the
language of *Lear*, the tendency is to repetitions that
accumulate intensity ("Speak. Nothing, my lord. Nothing! Nothing. Nothing will come of nothing. Speak
again." "Howl, howl, howl!" "Never, never, never,
never, never!" "Kill, kill, kill, kill, kill, kill!"). The method of the play is to expose us to more than we thought

we could take, and thus to make us acutely aware of all the phenomena associated with taking it, including physical exhaustion and the coining of platitudes. In a sense Lear is a play of competitions. Consider the number of times when characters are presented trying to outdo each other in extreme or strange activities. There is a very formal competition in filial affection at the play's beginning, as well as Lear's competition with the storm, in which he is seen "contending with the fretful elements," striving "to out-scorn/ The to-and-fro-conflicting wind and rain." Lear competes with Edgar in nakedness as well as madness. There is a sexual competition between Regan and Goneril over Edmund. The two daughters also have a habit of competing in bloody-mindedness:

REGAN
We shall further think of it.
GONERIL
We must do something, and i' th' heat.
(I, i, 311-12)

GONERIL
What need you five and twenty, ten, or five? . . .
REGAN
What need one?   (II, iv, 264-66)

REGAN
Hang him instantly.
GONERIL
Pluck out his eyes.   (III, vii, 4-5)

The chivalric trial-by-combat in the last scene is another formal competition, of a more conventional type—even disconcertingly so. Suddenly we are in the presence of Spenserian, fairy-tale, happy-ending-style combat (with Edgar, having advanced through a series of improvements in dress, now "fair and warlike" in armor). And at the very end one has a sense that a terrible endurance contest is going on. Gloucester's heart bursts between extremes of joy and grief. Under the same stress Kent's heart is cracking too, but he hangs on gamely, while everyone seems to agree with Edgar that Lear has borne the most—none of these sufferers (nor, we are assured, any future competitors) will be able to match him.

The last twist of the accumulative pattern is of course the moment which Bradley[3] quite correctly singles out as containing the most likely "moral" of *King Lear*:

ALBANY
The gods defend her! . . .
Enter Lear with Cordelia dead in his arms.
(v, iii, 256)

At this point Kent raises the question that perplexed Tate and the eighteenth century editors: "Is this the promis'd end?" Now, there is nothing that makes us feel more superior to this era than its "improvements" of *King Lear*. But Tate's version and Johnson's approval of it show that they at least felt the play's essential quality: that it is nearly or perhaps wholly unbearable. We may well ask ourselves whether our eagerness to perform the full text represents openness to its pain or rather a superior capacity to be untouched by it. Black comedy is a grim vision of life, but it is no substitute for black tragedy. Samuel Johnson apprehended the power of blackness as deeply as any man, and that is why he could not bring himself to reread the last act for years. If the play is presented with anything like its true horror, Kent's question should become our own. He is referring to the promised end of Doomsday, of course, but since we have clearly reached the final scene, the other meaning is present too. Is this the way the play is supposed to end?

It is perhaps especially shattering for Kent, because

[3] *Shakespearean Tragedy* (New York, 1955), p. 260.

he has been promising us a different end, or at least part of an ending, for a long time. He gets a lot of dramatic play out of the fact that he intends to stay in disguise until the right moment. He makes frequent allusions to his real identity. This to the Gentleman:

> I'll bring you to our master Lear,
> And leave you to attend him. Some dear cause
> Will in concealment wrap me up awhile.
>
> (IV, iii, 52-54)

This to Cordelia when she urges him to change out of his servant's garb:

> Pardon, dear madam;
> Yet to be known shortens my made intent.
> My boon I make it, that you know me not
> Till time and I think meet. (IV, vii, 8-11)

And he then goes on to reply gnomically to the Gentleman's rumor that he, Kent, is in Germany (90-92).

Now what is this dear cause that he has in mind? It can't be attending on Lear, since he leaves the Gentleman to do that. It can't be his political mission to Cordelia because he has completed it. As far as we can tell he spends his time after his last speech to Cordelia wandering around the battlefield . . . but such speculation is an exercise in the wrong kind of Bradleyism. As members of the audience we know exactly what his dear cause and made intent is—he wants to reveal himself to his master as part of the grand finale. He encounters unexpected difficulties, however, because Lear has other things on his mind:

KENT

O my good master!

LEAR

Prithee, away.

EDGAR

'Tis noble Kent, your friend.

CHAPTER VII

LEAR

A plague upon you, murderers, traitors all!
I might have sav'd her.   (v, iii, 267-70)

Lear soon recognizes him, but it is not a "recognition"
in the technical dramatic sense:

Who are you?
Mine eyes are not o' th' best. I'll tell you straight.
. . . Are you not Kent?   (278-82)

Lear does not realize that Kent has been masquerading
as Caius. Kent makes an effort to establish the connection, but fails to produce the expected theatrical
surprise. Lear blankly accepts the news:

KENT
The same,
Your servant Kent. Where is your servant Caius?
LEAR
He's a good fellow, I can tell you that;
He'll strike, and quickly too. He's dead and rotten.
KENT
No, my good lord; I am the very man,—
LEAR
I'll see that straight.
KENT
—That, from your first of difference and decay,
Have follow'd your sad steps—
LEAR
You are welcome hither.
(282-89)

It is as if Orestes should reveal himself to Electra and
she should say, "Oh, hello Orestes." The tragedy has
outstripped Kent's scenario. He really can't accompany
Lear here, no matter how he tries. The end he has
promised us has to be scrapped. It is all yet another
device (like Edgar's precise description of the abyss for
Gloucester's benefit) for giving us a sense of having

gone further than we could have expected and, consequently, as far as we can go.

The scene is designed, as the play has been, to make us feel that we are seeing the worst. Edmund's effort to save Lear and Cordelia, for example, should not be slighted in production. It provides a very important little arc of activity. At this point all the evil characters have been expelled from power. They are either dead or dying, and the dying Edmund is no longer malign. For the first time in the play, no one means any harm. Yet the suffering of the good continues to increase. We may remember that the whole sequence has been preceded by Edgar's triumphant announcement, "The gods are just."

The question of what is worst naturally reflects the question of what is bad. All bad or unpleasant experiences reawaken our primitive disappointment at the discovery that we are not identical with nature. Cordelia's fault in the first scene is precisely this. She insists, very simply, that she is not identical with what Lear wishes her to be. Her father believes that "nature" ("where nature doth with merit challenge") will express itself in a declaration of total love. Cordelia's refusal smashes this root conviction, one that a childish and flattered ruler might well retain—one that in some measure we all do. It is a belief that dies hard and painfully because it exempts us from suffering:

> They told me I was everything.
> (IV, vi, 106)

The early scenes of the play keep this idea of totality active in our minds almost as much as the idea of "nothing":

I love you more than word can wield the matter;
Dearer than eye-sight, space, and liberty;
Beyond what can be valued, rich or rare;
No less than life, with grace, health, beauty, honour;

As much as child e'er lov'd, or father found;
A love that makes breath poor, and speech unable:
Beyond all manner of so much I love you.
(I, i, 56-62)

Sure, I shall never marry like my sisters
To love my father all. (I, i, 105-106)

I gave you all. (II, iv, 253)

One question the play probes is, what are we if we are not all? Lear rapidly experiences worse things than Cordelia's rejection, but it is a movement from worst to worse. The very beginning of the play has plunged him from all to nothing.

The drama advances us deeper and deeper into nothing, but we experience moments of remarkable illumination along the way, of "feeling," to use another word the play stresses at crucial moments. At its end, the state is exhausted, it can only be "sustained" like so much misery or a wounded body. The remaining characters are exhausted too. Kent is dying. The final image must be of Albany and Edgar helping him from the stage, "sustaining" him between them. All they have left is the memory of what they have seen and felt, and by this time seeing and feeling are words charged with meaning for us.

Albany has made an effort to play the role of the conventional leader who mops up capably and efficiently at the end of a tragedy. He attempts the familiar concluding message of a Fortinbras or a Malcolm: "Let's get this nation moving again":

you, to your rights,
With boot, and such addition as your honours
Have more than merited. All friends shall taste
The wages of their virtue, and all foes
The cup of their deservings.
(v, iii, 300-304)

But this too is a promised end that has to be scrapped.
Once more the play moves from a summing up to insistence on the unbearable. Albany breaks off and cries,
"O, see, see!" It is this kind of contrast that Edgar has
in mind when he says:

> Speak what we feel, not what we ought to say.
> . . . We that are young
> Shall never see so much, nor live so long.
> (324-26)

Lear at the end is seeing and feeling with a peculiar
intensity, asking questions we cannot answer and seeing things we cannot see. Just as with Edgar's description of the abyss, we cannot quite see all—"the deficient
sight" fails. "Look on her, look, her lips,/ Look there,
look there!" We have gone as far as we can go; we almost see but we can't see. Nothing, as Kent has said,
almost sees miracles but misery.

Cordelia has defined her relation to her father as a
bond:

> I love your Majesty
> According to my bond; no more nor less.
> (I, i, 94-95)

Her statement has a richness that dominates memory.
On the one hand it is a simple plain proposition that
has the ring of truth and common sense, standing out
with its "no more nor less" against the all-or-nothing
absolutes of the first scene. But it also resists and
teases our understanding; it is a line that the rest of
the play must make clear. "Bond," whether in its legal
or material sense (and both are present here), is a
word of double significance; a bond brings things together, but it sets up limits too. At the moment Cordelia
makes her pronouncement, bonds seem to start breaking all over the stage. Lear curses his daughter, and
Kent's voice is heard calling his king mad and blind.
("See better, Lear.") It is Cordelia's suggestion that

people are held together by bonds which are necessarily not limitless that starts Lear on the course that eventually leads him to call on Nature to destroy all bonds. But Cordelia's love, if it is less than all, is more than nothing. Under the extreme pressures of reduction, Lear explores the "needs" of humanity, the bonds that the art of our necessities throws into sharp relief.

From the audience's point of view Lear is what Cordelia at one point calls him, a "perdu," a sentry posted in an exposed position, a lost man, but one on whom we depend to hold and patrol our furthest advances into threatening territory. And this helps to explain and define what both actors and audience must undergo if they are to possess the play. By its end we should have been made to see and feel a succession of competing shocks, tortures, and degradations whose rhythm we recognize as bound up with our own abiding misery, which we make every effort to ignore or to convert into something less troublesome: our experience of the nothing that comes of not being all.

Cordelia's death has kept us from the last temptation to falsify, to believe that because goodness exists life is essentially good. Pain remains in spite of endurance, in spite of grace. But what we have seen and felt remains, too. Cordelia has loved Lear according to her bond, and we have been made to see and feel that bond, and the bond between Lear and the Fool, between Edgar and Gloucester, between Lear and the naked wretches who endure the storm, between ourselves and, through the bodies of the actors, the suffering body of humanity.

VIII

Coriolanus and the Crowd

IF IT IS worthwhile to study our relation to the actor's specific tasks and triumphs in a play as part of Shakespeare's design, it is equally valuable to pay careful attention to his management of groups of actors, to what might be called the play's large-scale choreography. Anyone who cares to examine the deployment of groups on the stage in the first scene of *Titus Andronicus*, say, or the funeral processions of *1 Henry VI*, or the escalating scenes of violence in *2 Henry VI* will be aware that Shakespeare from the first was able to handle masses of men in movement on the stage so as to provide clarity of structure, depth of emotion, and a heightened sense of issue for his audience. This chapter will consider a single example of this technique, one that has far-reaching significance for its play.

In *Coriolanus*, crowds, armies, and groups of people in general are used as part of a recurring choreographical motif which critically affects our sense of the hero and his situation. The device is also helpful in overcoming a difficulty which might be considered inherent to the play's dramatic material: the problem of monotony. *Coriolanus* is not a bore, but the ingredients for boredom are there. The defining energy of the play might well strike a reader as constricted and abrasive. The variation of mood, locale, intensity, and action is narrow. Political argument, or rather the exchange of political invective, is nearly incessant. Though the characterizations are among Shakespeare's sharpest and most economical, there is little in them to charm, and even the number of unique specimens offered does little to relieve the sense of a fixed monotony of contention. Again, it is narrowness rather than unpleasantness that puts the reader off.

More important, the impression of monotony extends even to the title role. If one thinks simply of the variety of response to be expected from the hero, a comparison not only with Hamlet but even Macbeth is all to Coriolanus's disadvantage. Indeed his tragedy depends on the fact that the people around him know precisely what his response to certain critical stimuli will be. As Antony is the most unpredictable, Coriolanus is the most predictable of men. He is like the kind of mechanical toy that was the subject of a wave of jokes some years ago—the Coriolanus doll: wind him up and he rages:

> Being once chaf'd, he cannot
> Be rein'd again to temperance.
>
> (III, iii, 27-28)

The Tribunes play upon this predictable response, and find it even easier to discredit him than they have guessed. And Aufidius not only uses the same method of simple insult to provoke Coriolanus's final outburst, but he begins with the identical triggering word—"traitor"—the Tribunes have used to precipitate his banishment. There is even something predictable about the crucial reaction to his mother's plea to spare Rome. Though the moment on stage is pivotal to the plot and very different in character from almost anything in the rest of the play, Coriolanus's decision does not seem to issue from any new insight or resolution. Rather, as when she persuades him to face the Tribunes in the market place (III, ii), Volumnia prevails because Coriolanus cannot finally disobey his mother. Her appeals and his reaction to them are virtually the same as in the earlier scene. We are not likely to feel that there is an elusive heart to Coriolanus's mystery which we are defied to pluck out. Toward the end of the play when he is compared to an engine:

When he walks, he moves like an engine, and the ground shrinks before his treading. He is able to pierce a corslet with his eye; talks like a knell, and his hum is a battery. He sits in his state, as a thing made for Alexander. . . .   (v, iv, 18-24)

we recognize that though this may represent some change in character to his friends, it is at most a change in degree, not kind. He is no less a "noble thing" —and no more—at the end than the beginning.

The image of a huge clanking engine, both terrific and apparently monotonous in its effects, is appropriate not only to Coriolanus but to his play. Slamming, regular, machine-like confrontation, verbal and physical, political and military, is the great characteristic both of the action and the hero. Variety of heart and habit, surprise, repose—all things, in short, that might easily alleviate our sense of constriction and monotony —would seem to be the victims of this impulse, and it is part of the play's meaning that they are. This is a play, for once, in which we must not be allowed the sense of selves breaking out into variety, abundance, or fresh illumination. And yet, the play is not boring. Its impulse somehow manifests itself in action that any well-served audience will recognize as of the satisfyingly tragic type. To explain how the apparent narrowness and monotony of the play can be an aspect of a profoundly stimulating theatrical design (and why the spectacle, which is in many ways as repetitious as Coriolanus's reactions, is not itself boring), to get, in short, at the real bite and rhythm of the play, we have to turn to its characteristic *activity*—what we principally see happening on the stage.

In *Antony and Cleopatra*, our sense of the main character depends more on what is said about him than on what he does. Most of the crucial battle action takes place offstage. Antony's flight from the Roman world to Egypt likewise takes place out of our sight and hurriedly. In *Coriolanus*, on the other hand, the hero is in the thick of battle, politically and militarily, to an extent that must have put great demands on the resources of Shakespeare's theater. His military exploits are abundantly praised, as Antony's are, but we are also shown them in great and exciting detail, throughout much of a particularly busy first act. The reason for this is not to convince us that Coriolanus is a military hero, but rather to establish a pattern of activity that relates Coriolanus to the people around him in a way that crucially affects our response to the entire play.

The play begins with a mob hunting Coriolanus; at the end a mob kills him. The mob changes its identity and character as the play goes on (though it will very likely be composed of the same acting personnel throughout). Sometimes it is Volscian, sometimes Roman, a street crowd in one scene, an army in another, but the nature of its involvement with Coriolanus remains constant. To be more precise, the crowd's relation to Coriolanus oscillates quickly and regularly between the poles of attack and adoration. What is important here is not so much the idea implied by the relationship (the crowd is fickle, Coriolanus is great and unbearable)—the repetition would be excessive if this were the only point to be made—but that its physical impact is repeated and overwhelming.

A brief survey of the crowd scenes bears this out. The battle before the walls of Corioli rages back and forth. Marcius leads his troops in a charge; they are beaten off the stage and leave him alone. He attacks the Volscians again and once more his troops abandon him (I, iv, 45ff). He is shut inside the gates (offstage—though the gates are visible), apparently to be slaughtered. He reemerges, "bleeding, assaulted by the enemy." Having been trapped by a crowd, he is now liberated by one. His soldiers extricate him, follow him, and enter the city. Next we see him cheered and adulated by the Roman troops:

*They all shout and wave their swords, take him up
in their arms, and cast up their caps.*

(I, vi, 75)

In I, viii he is surrounded by an attacking group of
Volscians and fights them off. In I, ix he is cheered
again:

They all cry, "Marcius! Marcius!" *cast up their caps
and lances.*

The political scenes continue the pattern. In II, ii Coriolanus is surrounded by the Senate, and though praised,
he responds as if attacked. He tries to leave and finally
breaks away. The next scene finds him once more the
center of a crowd's attention. We see the citizens approaching Coriolanus a few at a time, as he stands in
the gown of humility. He seeks to win their favor, and
they, for their part, treat him with deference, even
admiration, but he cannot conceal his distaste for
them, and after he has left they quickly form into a
mob once more and go off angrily to confront him.
Act III, scene i develops into a street brawl with Coriolanus at the center:

CITIZENS

Down with him! down with him!

SENATOR

Weapons, weapons, weapons!
     They all bustle about Coriolanus, [crying]
Tribunes! Patricians! Citizens! What, ho!
Sicinius! Brutus! Coriolanus! Citizens! . . .

CORIOLANUS

     I'll die here.
          Drawing his sword.
There's some among you have beheld me fighting;
Come, try upon yourselves what you have seen me . . .

BRUTUS

Lay hands upon him.

113

COMINIUS
Help Marcius, help;
You that be noble, help him, young and old!
CITIZENS
Down with him, down with him!
In this mutiny, the Tribunes, the
Aediles, and People, are beat in.
(184-229)

In III, iii he appears once more before the crowd; it calls for his banishment, and cheers when he denounces the citizenry and leaves the stage.

When Coriolanus goes over to the enemy in IV, v, he is harassed by a group of serving men (the parts may be doubled by, say, the first, second, and third Citizens from the earlier crowds) who later praise him extravagantly. Finally, in the last scene, he returns to "great shouts of the People," but within seventy lines the people are calling for his death:

Tear him to pieces! Do it presently!—He kill'd my son!—
My daughter!—He kill'd my cousin Marcus!—He kill'd
my father!   (V, vi, 121-24)

The raging action of the crowds around Coriolanus provides a sustaining dramatic impulse for the play, as well as obviously embodying its central situation. It also accounts for the fact that the impulse is ultimately and very clearly tragic. In *The Story of the Night,*[1] John Holloway has seen deeply into the relation between the Shakespearean tragic hero and the multitude, and his insight is useful here. Holloway develops the idea that all the major tragedies exhibit a pattern of action which relates the hero to those around him while at the same time isolating and finally sacrificing him. The

[1] Lincoln, 1961. The passages quoted in this paragraph are from pp. 123 and 130.

pattern is more emphatically marked in some plays than in others, but present to some degree in all. As Holloway points out, *Coriolanus* is a preeminent example of "the transformation . . . of cynosure at once into a victim and a monster," hunted and hounded by those who had honored or professed to adore him before. Though Holloway is concerned with the dramatic significance of "sacrificial victims," his analysis of *Coriolanus* is confined for the most part to the appearance of this motif simply as a subject of discourse in the play. Aside from his acute observation that "the death of Coriolanus is almost as much a *sparagmos* of the ritual victim by the whole social group as was possible on stage," he limits himself to what is *said* about Coriolanus, to spoken descriptions of his reception by the people and to comments Coriolanus himself makes. Any survey of the events on stage makes it clear, however, that the relation of Coriolanus and the crowd is much more than a theme for reflection; it is a driving pulse of activity, designed to be powerfully registered by the audience. Attention to the spectacle suggests, in fact, that while the "transformation of cynosure into a victim and a monster" may be a fair summary of the plot, what we experience in scene after scene is not a gradual change from one state to the other, but rather a sort of traumatic oscillation between the two poles. Crowds alternately celebrate and revile Coriolanus, they adore and menace him, they gather about him and disperse, while he constantly calls them together and spurns them from him, shows them his wounds but doesn't show them, offers them his body and takes it away.

One of Shakespeare's departures from his source indicates how important this pattern is. Plutarch's account of the episode in which Coriolanus first penetrates the walls of Corioli is as follows, in North's translation:

Fewe had the hartes to followe him. Howbeit Martius being in the throng among the enemies, thrust him selfe into the gates of the cittie, and entred the same emong them that fled, without that any one of them durst at the first turne their face upon him, or els offer to staye him. But he looking about him, and seeing he was entred the cittie with very fewe men to helpe him, and perceyving he was environned by his enemies that gathered round about to set apon him: dyd things then as it is written, wonderfull and incredible, aswell for the force of his hande, as also for the agillitie of his bodie, and with a wonderfull corage and valliantnes, he made a lane through the middest of them, and over-threwe also those he layed at: that some he made ronne to the furthest parte of the cittie, and other for feare he made yeld them selves, and to let fall their weapons before him.[2]

In the play, all of Coriolanus's men refuse to follow him.[3] ("Fool-hardiness; not I . . . To th' pot, I warrant him.") More important, he does not triumph easily. The change allows him not only to be sharply isolated from his troops, but to reappear surrounded by attacking enemies. The main point of the alteration lies with the choreography—it allows for a systole and diastole of crowds with Coriolanus at the center.

Coriolanus, whether among crowds or not, moves almost perpetually through an atmosphere of narrow, chafing, machine-like conflict. Few scenes of the play that involve him are free of real clash, and the sense of incessant rough conflict is sustained and kept playing constantly on our nerves by the play's verse:

[2] *Narrative and Dramatic Sources of Shakespeare*, ed. Geoffrey Bullough, v (London, 1964), 512.

[3] Coriolanus's entry alone—though not his men's refusal—may have been suggested by Philemon Holland's translation of Livy. (See Bullough, v, 489. But cf. Livy himself, II, 33.)

> For your wants,
> Your suffering in this dearth, you may as well
> Strike at the heaven with your staves as lift them
> Against the Roman state, whose course will on
> The way it takes, cracking ten thousand curbs
> Of more strong link asunder than can ever
> Appear in your impediment.   (1, i, 68-74)

The language of *Coriolanus* is terse, elliptical, rapid, studded with invective, dense; it suggests quick, tough activity, bleakness rather than lushness. Even when meanings appear that invite rounded periods or advert to vital process, phrases are preferred that convey a rattling, harsh, eroding, or combative impression.

As Wilson Knight has noted,[4] much of the imagery is drawn from ordinary life and used in a way that suggests a Roman atmosphere far different from the imperial one of *Antony and Cleopatra*: this is early Republican Rome, just after the expulsion of the Tarquins, more a provincial town than a great capital. Taken as a whole, the imagery, diction, and rhythm emphatically sustain a feeling of energetic but rather mean conflict that is fundamental to the play.

Coriolanus is of course peculiarly suited to this atmosphere. His personality is firmly and finely etched. There is little in the way of explanation that need be added to the composite portrait modern critics have extracted of him. Still, the relation of this "character" to the drama of which it is only a part may be made clearer if it is seen against the dominant activity of the play. Though it is misleading to call the portrait satirical (our full involvement in the battle scenes—obviously intended—would in itself preclude this; they would be dull if controlled by satire), surely no tragic hero is presented in a more critical fashion. Antony

4 "The Royal Occupation: An Essay on Coriolanus," *The Imperial Theme*, 3d ed. (London, 1951), pp. 154-98.

117

and Cleopatra's first entrance is carefully framed by disapproving comment, but their speeches subvert the criticism (though without contradicting it). In the first scene of *Coriolanus*, however, not only are the citizens violently opposed to the hero, speaking lines that gain validity as the play progresses ("He did it to please his mother, and to be partly proud"), but his own opening lines more than reinforce their criticism. Menenius, having with great difficulty succeeded in calming the angry crowd, greets him effusively:

> Hail, noble Marcius! (167)

Coriolanus answers:

> Thanks. What's the matter, you dissentious rogues,
> That, rubbing the poor itch of your opinion,
> Make yourselves scabs? (168-70)

The reply is, or should be, shocking. It must make the audience gasp if it is not to laugh.

As a person, Coriolanus is immature, rigid to the point of being brittle. Aufidius's final taunt of "Boy" is perfectly gauged. He is quick to rage, easily put out of countenance, and his anger at being praised is less modest than pathological. As the play progresses it becomes increasingly clear that he is deficient in some essential capacity for human intercourse. His mother is a monster, his wife a significantly shadowy and melancholy figure. The language of affection in the play is reserved for descriptions of war and enemies; and Coriolanus seems bound to others only by the relations of the battlefield, which like the emotions of the crowd, are passionate but easily reversed.

This basic immaturity helps explain another notable element in the presentation of his character: a lack of inwardness that is one of the most theatrically awkward aspects of the part. Antony lets a rich range of sensibility play over his situation. Coriolanus does not. Indeed, Menenius, Aufidius, and any number of others provide a wider view of Coriolanus's possible responses to the events of the play than he does—and a deeper sounding of the feelings they may be presumed to evoke. When Coriolanus goes over to the enemy, for example, the play, as Granville-Barker points out,[5] denies us any point of swing. It is the sort of critical transition marked in *Julius Caesar, Hamlet, Macbeth, Othello,* and *Antony and Cleopatra* by analytic and emotionally rich soliloquies. Coriolanus's soliloquy, however, simply informs us of a *fait accompli.* We are not allowed to experience the actual moment of choice; the inwardness of the process is concealed from us. The crucial scene with Volumnia is likewise restricted. Considered in isolation simply for the dramatic opportunities it offers, as a piece an actor might use at an audition, say, it is disappointing. It would not be hard to imagine a livelier treatment of the material. The hero's articulate response to the great peripety is rudimentary, purely external. And of the scene's most surprising result—his decision to return to Corioli rather than Rome—he gives us nothing but the bare announcement of intent.

Out of dramatic context, the scene is opaque to the point of dullness. Encountered in the midst of the play's furious activity, it is poignantly clear—though it remains perhaps the most difficult of Shakespeare's great tragic scenes to perform effectively. The point of course is that nothing is articulated; the climax is a stage direction:

> *He holds her by the hand, silent.*
> (v, iii, 182)

If Coriolanus could speak here, he would not be Coriolanus and the tableau would lose its significance. Dramatically, it is a silent moment in a noisy play, a point

---

[5] *Prefaces to Shakespeare,* II (Princeton, 1947), 156.

of stasis in the churning choreography. It is unique, too, in that it is a moment of simple affection. That this should seem dull in isolation admits of no surprise. A son holds his mother's hand, having agreed to act kindly toward her and toward his wife, child, and city. A son and a mother; the moment is opaque if only because it is banal—but what a mother and what a son! If Coriolanus has been a "thing," a machine, he has been set in motion ("wound up" might be more accurate) at least partly by his upbringing; and if he has tried to become a greater and greater machine as his encounters with the populace have irritated him, now his one gesture toward something that is not mechanism—a response he cannot control (and cannot, it would seem, even begin to express), a gesture which is banal because it is in every man's character and inarticulable because it is not in Coriolanus's—must destroy him.

In the later phases of his career, Shakespeare becomes increasingly interested in the irreducible and minimal aspects of the sounded self. "Simply the thing I am/ Shall make me live," asserts Parolles; and *Macbeth* and *King Lear* raise the question of what, minimally, is the thing that makes a man a man. Coriolanus takes the process a step further, for now the hero's self itself is minimal, and not simply the circumstances in which it is placed. Under the strain of his drama, Coriolanus reveals a hidden self that is almost hollow—but not quite. He is perhaps ashamed of it as he is of his wounds; like them, it is the most human thing about him. No man is a machine, after all. The Roman warrior who has been bred and trained so true that he seems mechanical still possesses a live human center, but in Coriolanus's case it is sadly stunted, nearly mute. The terrible fact, at the moment Volumnia's appeal finally touches him, is not that his action now must commit him to death—that was to be expected—but that he has no *inner* options either, not even Macbeth's capacity for imagining what he has become. The meagerness of his sounded self allows him only negative expression. Beyond agreeing not to sack his city, not to do what he has sworn, he can only express a blank, wondering awareness of his fate:

> O my mother, mother! O!
> You have won a happy victory to Rome;
> But, for your son,—believe it, O believe it—,
> Most dangerously you have with him prevail'd,
> If not most mortal to him. (v, iii, 185-89)

The pathos of Coriolanus's silent gesture lies in the machine's discovering at the moment of its greatest humanity that it is far too much of a machine, tragically limited by the forces that have created its excellence.

As the silence of the scene contrasts with the noise of the play, the noise of the following scene differs from the play's other noises. The crowd's response to Volumnia's return to Rome is a new one. The music is other than martial; hautboys are played and "sackbuts, psalteries, and fifes,/ Tabors and cymbals" are referred to. For once in the play no greasy, stinking caps are thrown into the air. The imagery, too, suggests fertility and abundance to a degree unmatched in any other scene. Wilson Knight has with great insight drawn attention to the importance of these images of music and abundance,[6] but this is only half the story. It must also be observed that the verse carefully keeps these new impulses within the recognizable tone of the play as a whole:

> Good news, good news! The ladies have prevail'd,
> The Volscians are dislodg'd, and Marcius gone.
> A merrier day did never yet greet Rome,
> No, not th' expulsion of the Tarquins. . . .
> Where have you lurk'd, that you make doubt of it?

[6] *The Imperial Theme*, p. 197.

Ne'er through an arch so hurried the blown tide,
As the recomforted through th' gates. Why, hark
    you!
The trumpets, sackbuts, psalteries, and fifes,
Tabors and cymbals and the shouting Romans,
Make the sun dance.   (v, iv, 43-54)

Except perhaps for the sixth of these lines, the spare
and counter quality of the play's cadence and diction
prevails. One has only to think of *Antony and Cleopatra* to realize how easily Shakespeare could have
opened the scene out, if he had wished, to accommodate a full-blown sensuousness of expression. It would
have required a marked shift in verse style, but he
does not shrink from such theatrically potent effects
at crucial moments elsewhere.[7] Here, however, he aims
for a tone that might best be described as "a shrill
piping of plenty." The chafing narrowness of this con-
tentious Roman world is suddenly full of a kind of relief it has not experienced before—but the world has not
shed its limiting identity any more than Coriolanus has
escaped his. "Unshout the noise that banish'd Marcius,"
is the giddy cry, but it is still a noisy one and, as we
know, the confidence is misplaced. Rome, like Coriolanus, is locked in its instinctual penury, transmitting
to us at this instant only by the barest hints the out-
lines of a power toward life it does not really possess.
The poetic effect is subtle, but profoundly attuned to
the larger movement of the play. The slight verbal and
musical expansion in an otherwise severely restricted
spectrum suggests the joy a different kind of heroic
self might bring to a different kind of nurturing state,
but it keeps active our keen awareness of the difference. On a small scale, this reflects what *Coriolanus*'s
choreography of violent action has been doing for the
play as a whole: bringing together the play's political

[7] As for example in *As You Like It*, iv, iii, 76-78; or *1 Henry
IV*, iv, i, 97-110; or *Macbeth*, i, vi, 1-10.

issues and the character of the hero in a form that suggests both splendor and barrenness. The movement of the crowds both traps and exalts the man at the center. Coriolanus draws his life from them; he defines his heroism and integrity by endlessly clashing with them and calling them together. In spite of their awesome energies, neither he nor Rome can be genuinely free for celebration, affection, variety, and warmth. Their exciting, sterile energy sustains and limits them.

The final scene, set at Corioli, also ends in a new civic mood. After the murder, Aufidius's emotions reverse themselves like any mob's, and are echoed in eulogy and dead march. In this new calm Coriolanus's terrible, narrow force can be honored without the threat of reversal and clash. The exaltation which I think we feel at the end comes from three sources: the exciting energy of hero and crowd; the sudden change of mood in Corioli; the Roman joy we have witnessed in the previous scene. In his barren and splendid way, Coriolanus has managed to transcend his limitations. His sacrifice has brought to Rome a moment of shared human pleasure none of his other triumphs could possibly achieve.

IX

The Winter's Tale
and
The Tempest

I REMEMBER an admired teacher saying to his class that there is a point in life when we discover that nature has lost interest in us. We who heard him were undergraduates, and though we must have counted this among his grand and gnomic statements, I imagine none of us had a very clear understanding of what he meant. If we thought about it at all, we probably considered that he was referring to some death-bed phase of human existence, a phenomenon of extreme old age. Of course it *was* a phase radically remote from our kingly state of youth, but near enough, alas, in clock-time. Past thirty, one begins to see what he had in mind. Life goes on, health and pleasure too, and no immediate limit, with luck, seems to be set on it. But one has ceased to be a growing thing, one is not being fattened up, one no longer gains strength each year no matter what one's carelessness. One follows "physical fitness" programs as if to make up with a personal concern for the concern nature has withdrawn. We become "masters of our fate," lacking a better master. Nature has lost interest, without malevolence and practically without a sign.

Nature loses interest in us, but nature never loses interest in life. The idea is important to an understanding of the vision of Shakespeare's last plays. Human life is tragic, but life itself is not. The revolution of time brings in new flowers and a new generation. Daughters grow up and marry. The great destructive forces, like the sea, are also indifferently restorative, restorative enough to keep growth happening. Births succeed on deaths. We are continually being reminded of the process by which loss leads to restoration and death to birth, in which growth is juxtaposed with destruction. One effort these plays make is to find dramatic equivalents for this endless superhuman recreation, and one of the ways they do this is by the transformation of symbols of tragedy, the specifically individual and limited encounter with natural process.

At the same time, Shakespeare seems concerned with the ways in which the individual comes somehow to participate in the superhuman restorative impulse of nature, the way in which the endlessly renewing force gets incorporated into moments of human life; he seems to seek out gestures or trains of action that touch this spring of natural energy, that seem to restore to the tragic individual, if only momentarily, nature's interest in his life.

The gestures that the plays concentrate on are largely gestures of *kindness*—allowing "kind" its full Elizabethan range of meaning. "Kind" may of course refer to species or family, or to Nature either in general or the abstract; as an adjective it can mean "natural," "ready to love," "disposed to treat others well," "tender," "affectionate." All these have importance in Shakespeare. But each meaning tends toward the others, and it is this aggregate of meaning that concerns me here. For the notion of kind-ness is far more important to Shakespeare's work than even his recurrent use of "kind" might indicate. Broadly speaking, kindness refers to all the acts and states of soul that tend to establish or identify human ties. The bonds tested and discovered in *King Lear* measure kindness against evil; Coriolanus's self is finally sounded by an appeal to kindness. From the deep and easy courtesy of the young men of the early plays to the terrible parody of generosity in the second half of *Timon*, from the pilgrim decency of his young women in love to the minimal definitions of humanity in the later work, kindness, in this large sense, is one of Shakespeare's central subjects. But to call it a subject is still to do some injustice to the depth of its significance. It imparts to the poetry its own variety of tones and colorations. If a uniquely Shakespearean response to life had to be identified—beyond something like "negative capability"—one might well point to a certain recurrent sweetness of address and concern between characters, which even in the earliest plays gets introduced whenever possible. In general, Shakespeare's people are kinder to each other than their plays need them to be. The gentle music of considerateness seems always eager to come in. There is, too, an angry music that calls out for considerateness, for human-kindness where it has been denied (as in Lear's "O reason not the need" or Isabella's appeal to Angelo). Even the courtesy of lords to inferiors is tinged, wherever admissible, with a special thoughtfulness and warmth.

The climactic gestures of the four last plays reestablish important human relations, family ones particularly; they are gestures of sympathy and generosity—recognitions, reconciliations, pardons, reunions. What is restored is a harmony that involves the closest of human ties. The plays offer us emblems which suggest that a conformity exists between natural process and our deepest intuitions of human kindness. Their heroines are figures in whom nature is interested, and they are seen extending that interest to others. Thus, the recurrent image of these girls decked in flowers. In part they are goddesses of Nature, simply identified with the high energies of spring, with the life process; but they are also associated with art, with arranging flowers for various purposes, festive or commemorative. They have something individual to offer, something they make, which partakes of the natural restorative force. The flowers are natural, but they are in a sense the girls' own doing.

The last plays do not simply dwell on examples of kindness. They are concerned with the varieties of feeling inherent in the idea itself and our attraction to it, with our appetite for reconciliation and restoration, and—for our purposes perhaps most important of all— with the relation of kindness to certain types of theatrical experience. They develop a theme we saw broached in the sonnets: the relation between the pleasure we take in art and our longing for kindness, fairness, and truth in a world that cannot sustain them. They are in some sense commentaries on the role of kindness in life, on the reassurances we desire in our relation with nature that only artistic illusion or certain heartfelt gestures can convey. As *Hamlet* confronted us with the nature of our appetite for significant action, so these plays—particularly *The Tempest*—seem to confront us with our need for the powerful illusions of theatrical art and for the meanings they bear in our lives. The elaborate restorations of the final plays are all accompanied by striking reminders of their theatricality, by devices that make us specially conscious that as an audience we are partisans of the happy ending, that we admire the working out of intricate plots or the reunion of scattered families as we enjoy the recurrence of spring. Our life is not like that, but Life can be like that; we need to see life like that in order to be able to go on living. Moreover, our sense that life is not like that for us makes us connoisseurs of kindness and artists of kindness too.

The Winter's Tale

There are thus two cycles of life—what I have called the tragic (or individual) and the superhuman. The interplay between the two in human activity, especially imaginative activity, is something the last plays are particularly sensitive to, heighten our awareness of, depend on in us for the audience response that sustains them. Curiously enough, for this very reason it can be misleading to talk about the plays in terms of familiar dichotomies—life and art, youth and age, illusion and reality, tragedy and comedy, nature and nurture—though they obviously invite discussion along these lines. It is not so much the opposition between the two cycles or the yielding of one to the other or even the notion of an alliance between the two that is central to the dramatic experience of the four romances. What is more important is the movement between two modes of being, each equally real. Art, in these terms, is not something to be distinguished from life, but a way of moving from one apprehension of reality to another, of allowing the limited human cycle to appear to contain the unlimited.

At the end of *The Winter's Tale*, the audience is—as Leontes fears himself to be—"mock'd with art." We are, of course, moved and touched and deeply satisfied as well, but there is no doubt that at least in part the remarkable and elusive statue scene keeps us pleased by keeping us off balance. There is no explaining why Hermione has remained hidden all these years, if she has in fact been alive. True, there is dramatically no need for an explanation. We are not allowed to pause over the problem. But we are made aware there is a secret, and we are not let in on it. Hermione begins as a statue—that is a fact of the scene—and after an interval in which some charming and teasing hints are dropped (and in which we may or may not guess what is about to happen) she turns into a human being.

Now, it is obviously possible to talk about this scene in terms of the antinomy between life and art. Wilson Knight does this in his great essay,[1] and argues that

---

[1] " 'Great Creating Nature': an Essay on *The Winter's Tale*," *The Crown of Life* (London, 1948), pp. 76-128.

at the end art gives way to life, the scene pointing the contrast. There are limits even to the highest art, he observes, and when Hermione turns out to breathe, move and talk—to be alive—she goes beyond them. This approach, suggestive as it is, does not seem quite true to what I take to be the felt experience of the play. Admittedly we are touched, as so often in Shakespearean comedy, by a sense of limit in the final moments— a limit to our and the characters' pleasure and to the pleasures art can offer us. (This feeling is very important to the last plays, and I shall want to deal with it later on.) But we are not made to think of art as inadequate while we watch Hermione's transformation. The emphasis is much more on the triumphs of art—on Julio Romano's powers and on the power of this fantastic happy ending to please an audience. What we are likely to feel most strongly is the sense of having been carried by art, as so regularly in *The Winter's Tale*, into an unexpectedly rewarding corner of life.[2]

[2] William Matchett's brilliant essay, "Some Dramatic Techniques in 'The Winter's Tale,' " *Shakespeare Survey* 22 (1969), 93-107, makes a pertinent point: when Paulina draws back the curtain, the audience will respond to the fact that the statue is represented by an actor, and be in excited perplexity as to whether or not the live player represents a living person. I would further suggest that the audience will with some part of its mind be testing its wild surmise against clues in the play so far. ("Can it really be Hermione? But there have been no hints. Didn't Paulina say something . . . no, she has to be dead!") Our desire for miracle will thus work its way into our sense of the dramatic artifice. We want Hermione to be alive, but we've thought it—the play has insisted we think it—impossible. And now here is the play hinting that the impossible will occur. Simply to bring on Hermione alive would have fallen flat. It would have violated the flow of our expectations beyond repair. It is the hint, the pausing between life and death as we watch the live actor whose status is unclear, that makes the impossibility acceptable, because our anticipation becomes joined to it. The excitement is all the greater because its source is no image but the real thing—it's a question of what the play will *do*, not what it will represent, that initially moves us. It is pro-

CHAPTER IX

Earlier we have looked forward to the pleasure of a grand recognition scene and a happy ending. We have apparently been balked of the first, and surely the reason why the scene between the kings and their children takes place off-stage is to displace our own energy of expectation onto the last scene with its fantastic resurrection. Shakespeare has constructed elaborately satisfactory happy endings before, some even happier than this. But in *The Winter's Tale*, as in other romances, the very happiness of the ending becomes a dramatic subject; our desire for things turning out all right is engaged and exploited as an important part of our experience of the play. The happy ending is one of the kindnesses of art, a way of improving on life which, at its best, can somehow be true to life. In the language of the play, happy endings, unexpected good fortune, gracious gestures, personal charm can "crown" actions, events, even themselves. Life can, at instants, improve on itself by itself—can raise itself to a royal level, to a state that partakes of the more-than-human to an unusual degree. And though this crowning moment can come about through strokes of incred-

---

foundly fitting in this play that our reaction should pivot on the fact that actors are alive, and therefore less convincing as statues than as people. For actors in their art make an unmediated connection between the human and superhuman cycles. They are real bodies and as such beyond the limits of art, but while acting they are works of art and beyond the limits of life. They are alive and yet they cannot die—such is the great creating nature of the theater.

Matchett makes the point that the scene heightens our awareness of theatrical make-believe, but this leads him, like Wilson Knight, to stress the importance of art's limitations, here and in the play as a whole. But in *The Winter's Tale* art is no more limited than life. Indeed, if there is a contrast between art and life in the statue scene, Shakespeare provides it in the swift closing movement, when Paulina is given Camillo as a husband. This much life can do. But even by royal command, Leontes can only replace Antigonus, not restore him.

ible luck or artifice (as in the recovery of Perdita as it appears to the people in the play or the deliberately tricky last scene as it appears to *us*), it can also be recognized in the natural power a charming girl has to transform an ordinary action simply by performing it:

> What you do
> Still betters what is done. When you speak, sweet,
> I'd have you do it ever; when you sing,
> I'd have you buy and sell so, so give alms,
> Pray so; and for the ord'ring your affairs,
> To sing them too. When you do dance, I wish you
> A wave o' th' sea, that you might ever do
> Nothing but that; move still, still so,
> And own no other function. Each your doing,
> So singular in each particular,
> Crowns what you are doing in the present deeds,
> That all your acts are queens.
>
> (IV, iv, 135-46)

Florizel's language here, in praising Perdita, keeps before us the question of the curious interrelatedness of art and nature that has already been raised more than once in the sheep-shearing scene—particularly in the exchange between Polixenes and Perdita. Perdita, Florizel says, imparts an added quality to her own nature—"What you do still betters what is done." The sentence is very hard to paraphrase. Shakespeare has said it perfectly, and it can only be said perfectly to be said intelligibly. But he is describing a secular version of grace; Perdita betters her own nature in every act. She is like nature, like a wave of the sea, like Flora herself. She is dressed up in a pretty (and, we may guess, slightly naïve) pastoral costume to play the role of Nature, but she also *is* Nature to the degree that she shares with Nature at this moment a superabundance of vital charm. Her life at this point coincides with the superhuman cycle. It is her nature to better her own nature.

We cannot say exactly where Perdita's artifice leaves off and her nature begins; or rather her art is a mode of experiencing her own nature, of rendering it clear to herself and her audience. Perdita's youthful summer is as real as Polixenes' age, just as the flowers of winter or early spring are as real as summer flowers—though they are not the flowers of this season. We become aware that the famous opposites—art and nature, the desirable and the actual, kindness and truth—are being made to coincide not only in the figure of Perdita, but—with increasing force—in the design of the entire scene.

The scene is a remarkable mixture of artifice and realism. Indeed, they both seem to increase as the action develops. We have already observed the backstage preparations, as it were—the old man bustling about, Perdita commenting on her costume, getting the festivities under way, even discussing art and nature (artlessly) with Polixenes. Perdita and Florizel are involved in a "real" pastoral of their own, since they are both impersonating rustics, though Perdita only thinks she is "really" a shepherd's daughter, while Florizel only pretends to be a shepherd. Soon the local shepherds and shepherdesses begin to dance. The festivity increases and grows coarser and more realistic as Autolycus comes in with his ballads, and is in time followed by the "saltiers" ("if it be not too rough for some that know little but bowling, it will please plentifully"). If the earliest stage of the scene has made us intensely conscious of symbolic significance—of issues like art, grace, and nature, of Perdita as Flora or Proserpine—the entrance of Autolycus, heralded by the shepherd with his excited talk of the "decent" ballads that are so dirty, reminds us how true to life this sheep-shearing is. Here is a pedlar selling ribbons, inkles, caddises, cambrics, and lawn to hard-handed boys and girls. But at the same time we are aware of more and more "art" in the scene. Autolycus is peddling devices designed to add beauty to natural beauty, and he is selling works of art, ballads. The ballads, it should be noted, are about freaks of fertility in nature and are taken as true by the wondering shepherds—whose healthy appetite for the impossibly creative and restorative is as great as our own—or as Leontes' at the end of the play ("Let it be an art/Lawful as eating").

Autolycus's antics are succeeded by even more elaborate artifice. The characters on stage stop their singing and prepare to watch a ballet. The saltiers may be "rough," but they are very accomplished dancers; three of them have appeared before the king. We may assume that in their satyr-play they are more explicit and bawdy than even the off-color ballads Autolycus has brought to the fair, but they are also the high point of non-realistic presentation in the play—in that the whole audience is now aware that it is watching a dance. As at a ballet interlude in a musical or an opera, a degree of intense abstraction seizes the stage. So that the "realer" we get, the more "art" we are conscious of.

The reason why songs and dances like this may occur without strain at this point in the play is that a festival is taking place; it is an occasion of art, and everyone involved, like Perdita, is playing a role. But festivals of this sort are a response to nature, to the creating, restoring superhuman process. Their art is to put us in touch with the power of the process, to celebrate it, to release its energy in ourselves, to let us share in its greatness. Again, the art we observe in this scene seems to enhance our own nature, to better what we do, to bring its own participants some kind of grace; but it is an art that rises directly out of nature: it is man thrust into delighted imitation by the abundance of summer.

In the final scene we have an example of an art that vies with nature—that indeed turns out to be nature after all. As the scene happens to us, though, what we see is art turning into nature, and we delight in it. Denied the recognition scene, we are all the more ready for wonders. It all turns out like an old tale, as Shakespeare keeps reminding us in the last act; it is something to wonder at, something to want completed. We remember also that Mamillius began a tale and left it unfinished before he disappeared from the story to die. His was a winter's tale, a sad tale, and we realize that by an act of art the winter's tale has become a summer's tale. We are likely, however, to think of Mamillius at the play's end, and we certainly do think of Antigonus when a new husband is found for Paulina, a sufficient reminder that though we have it within ourselves to be genuinely in touch with great creating nature in moments of festivity, in youth, in gestures of reunion and restoration, in elaborate art like that of this play, the reason we wonder at these moments and experience them with joy and admiration is that our own nature commits us finally to the tragic pattern.

The poise, the balancing of perceptions and desires which the dramatic pattern achieves may be discerned in a more purely lyric form in Perdita's flower speeches in iv, iv:

Here's flowers for you;
Hot lavender, mints, savory, marjoram;
The marigold, that goes to bed wi'th' sun
And with him rises weeping. These are flowers
Of middle summer, and I think they are given
To men of middle age. You're very welcome.
CAMILLO
I should leave grazing, were I of your flock,
And only live by gazing.
PERDITA
Out, alas!
You'd be so lean, that blasts of January
Would blow you through and through. Now, my fair'st friend,
I would I had some flowers o'th' spring that might
Become your time of day; and yours, and yours,

That wear upon your virgin branches yet
Your maidenheads growing. O Proserpina,
For the flowers now, that frighted thou let'st fall
From Dis's waggon! daffodils,
That come before the swallow dares, and take
The winds of March with beauty; violets dim,
But sweeter than the lids of Juno's eyes
Or Cytherea's breath; pale primroses,
That die unmarried, ere they can behold
Bright Phoebus in his strength—a malady
Most incident to maids.   (103-25)

We have a sense, with the daffodils (as with Perdita herself and her appearance after three acts of Sicilian tragedy), of natural wonder braving the tragic world of winter and storm. Yet it is a world full of tragic possibilities for the individual. The marigolds that wake up in tears, the poor sheep in winter, and the pale primroses that die unmarried before the summer sun can reach them remind us of the pathetic characters who have not survived (Mamillius, Antigonus, and, at this point, Hermione). The catalog suggests the innocent vulnerability of the individual flower before the dread process of the seasons. From her vantage point at the height of youthful summer, Perdita provides a kind of tender reminiscence of the pathos of early spring and its struggle with winter. We remember that in *Pericles* and *Cymbeline*, when Shakespeare decks his heroines with flowers, the flowers are destined not for the living but for the dead. Perdita's kindness, like that of Marina and Imogen, resembles the kindness of festival or of dramatic art, the restoration in human action of natural warmth to the inevitable human winter in our bones.

We will do well in conclusion to recall how the play has begun. The dialogue between Archidamus and Camillo does more than furnish necessary exposition. It focuses on an exchange of courtesies, a mildly comic version of a type of kindness, which like the festival is a response to abundance. The courtesy is ornate yet genuine. We gather immediately that Sicily is, at least to a Bohemian, a remarkably sophisticated and opulent court; Archidamus grows a little silly talking about it:

Wherein our entertainment shall shame us we will be justified in our loves; for indeed—

CAMILLO
Beseech you,—

ARCHIDAMUS
Verily, I speak it in the freedom of my knowledge. We cannot with such magnificence—in so rare—I know not what to say. We will give you sleepy drinks, that your senses, unintelligent of our insufficience, may, though they cannot praise us, as little accuse us.

(I, i, 9-17)

He is trying to use all his art to match the courtesy he has found at the court, and the actor has a chance to show him stumbling with the effort. Both he and Camillo are dealing in the true kindness of polite speech, but the comedy makes us sensitive to its artifice, especially as the scene modulates into a jesting exchange when they talk about Mamillius:

ARCHIDAMUS
You have an unspeakable comfort of your young Prince Mamillius. It is a gentleman of the greatest promise that ever came into my note.

CAMILLO
I very well agree with you in the hopes of him. It is a gallant child; one that indeed physics the subject, makes old hearts fresh. They that went on crutches ere he was born desire yet their life to see him a man.

ARCHIDAMUS
Would they else be content to die?

CAMILLO
Yes; if there were no other excuse why they should desire to live.

136

ARCHIDAMUS

If the King had no son, they would desire to live on crutches till he had one.   (37-50)

They are making fun of the artificiality of the extremer tropes of their courteous and courtier-like speech. Yet the little joke they make in doing so has its own related resonance. Its point is that people are not content to die—they will find some reason to live. Here, hard upon our first impression of abundance breeding abundance, we have the first hint in the play of the individual pattern—the tragic pattern—measured against the larger restorative pattern of nature.

The Tempest

A director searching for keys to a production of *The Tempest* must begin with the atmosphere. The action of the play is notably free from suspense or impediment, a fact that is made clear almost from the start. In a sense it is as if the last scene of *The Winter's Tale* were now taken as province for an entire play—the formal slipping of a knot already not only loose but unfastened, under the control of a powerful benign enchantment. The quality of the enchantment is central, and that is why the atmosphere is primary. The play's events are less important than the way they are felt: how they are received by the characters, how they appear to us, and how they are related to the arts of theatrical illusion in general.

It is the characters who tell us (and tell the director) what life on Prospero's island feels like. There is a peculiar quality to the experience Prospero submits them to, and they give it very full expression. The play abounds in descriptions of its own atmosphere, and the dominant word is "strange." The word has its dangers for the director, as the tradition of over-gorgeous and extravagantly spectacular productions attests, but if the play's own sense of the word is inquired after, the difficulties can be avoided. *The Tempest* discusses its own strangeness at length, and provides any number of examples and images of its general mood and background. Most of the actors are called upon to respond frequently to the strangeness— one of its major acting problems, in fact, is finding responses that are acceptable, interesting, and sufficiently varied. And their responses form part of the play's distinctive pleasure, part of its attractive strangeness for us.

The Tempest has a word for this type of response— "wonder." To Ferdinand, Miranda is a wonder, and she applies the same term to all mankind. Prospero presents the two lovers as a "wonder," which he brings forth to delight his guests at the end of the play. Part of the comedy of ii, ii is that Caliban, Stephano, and Trinculo react with foolish wonder and fear to each other, and Caliban continues to believe that Stephano is a "wondrous" man. Ferdinand hits upon the *mot juste* for Prospero when he calls him a "wond'red father." Reinforcing the general impression of wonderment, variants (or subcategories) of wonder like "amazement" and "admiration" are frequently invoked.

The audience, then, must feel the strangeness and it must watch the characters responding to strangeness with wonder. The actors' varied solutions to the problems of response will involve us with the nature of wonder, whose exact quality must thus receive great emphasis in the play. What is wonder? In *The Tempest* it is always expressed as a sudden conviction that the world is better or more abundant than one thought, that there are marvelous transforming powers at work in it. The music Ferdinand hears makes him ready to accept Miranda as a goddess. What is strange in the play is the natural, wondrously transformed. Even unpleasantness reaches us accompanied by wonder, for a crucial part of the strangeness of the play's atmosphere (even more than of the island's) is the mood in which painful possibilities and experiences are communicated to the audience. There are no deaths in this play, no Mamillius or Antigonus, not even a Cloten with his head cut off or a Duke's nephew (as in *Twelfth Night*) who has lost his leg at sea. More important, the spectacle, music, and language usually allow us to see pain suspended and, as it were, held at a distance, modified by magic and by wonder.

The fire and thunder that Ariel brings aboard the King's ship is spectacular but harmless, and in his description of the storm oddness and strangeness diffuse even the apparent violence of the scene:

> I boarded the King's ship; now on the beak,
> Now in the waist, the deck, in every cabin,
> I flam'd amazement. Sometime I'd divide,
> And burn in many places. On the topmast,
> The yards and bowsprit, would I flame distinctly,
> Then meet and join. . . .
>   The King's son, Ferdinand,
> With hair up-staring,—then like reeds, not hair,—
> Was the first man that leap'd.
>   (I, ii, 196-214)

Ferdinand's expression is so precisely and picturesquely realized that the moment is essentially strange rather than terrible (nor is it, as it might be, funny). Ariel is not simply an etherealized Puck, and the pleasure of his speech is not that he treats his acts as mischief. He has "flam'd amazement," and the eagerness and pride of his account, which itself helps sustain the mood, reflects his sense of the wonder he has produced on shipboard. A few lines later, by imitating him, Ariel reduces Ferdinand's desolation to an odd and charming posture: "sitting,/ His arms in this sad knot" (223-24). And our earlier picture of the Prince is of course a caricature of wonder, his hair sea-changed like reeds to stand on end.

Even characters who experience pain directly transmit it to us as strangeness. Sorrow modulates into wonder in their speech. Alonso, convinced that his son has drowned, asks:

> O thou mine heir
> Of Naples and of Milan, what strange fish
> Hath made his meal on thee?
> (II, i, 111-13)

The actor who plays Leontes can give us the fullest and ugliest of jealousies; indeed his problem is that he must do so suddenly and compactly without destroying the illusion or the play. But Alonso, if he is to be fair to these lines, must create some gauze or filter between the audience and the full intensity of potential sorrow, or the strange fish will have to be thrown away.

This tone of transformed sorrow is particularly apparent in Ferdinand, whose mourning for his father is so affected by the strange music he hears that not only does it overcome his passionate sorrows, but his description has a kind of distant elegance to it, rather than the broken, irrational cadences, say, of Leontes. Prospero's island is a world in which the painful and tragic become something rich and strange. In production, however, the richness and strangeness has to be of a lightness that allows the audience to attend to the delicacy and charm of the individual elements, particularly the verse—in which we are aware of a constantly varied musicality remarkably close to real speech, remarkably characterized and released from formal regularity, but at the same time perhaps the most lyrical (and difficult to speak) of all the plays. Again, the sense of the natural made wondrous is essential.

If we think of the strangeness of the atmosphere as a kind of orchestration in which unpleasantness is scored so as to suggest wonder, oddness, and charm, there is one other voice in the consort that must be mentioned. Painful possibility may also appear in a tonality which, though still avoiding direct and full-bodied dolor, has a distinctly less blurry, elegant, or remote effect than the examples already given. In fact, it comes to us as something like an irritation, the suggestion of some kind of sharpness abrading the wondrous world. When characters in *The Tempest* are afflicted to the point of becoming upset, they usually suffer a certain kind of disturbance, mental or physical, not of the highest amplitude on the chart of pain, but definitely painful. It is nagging, persistent, pulsing. Difficulties affect their minds by beating in them:

> I pray you, sir,
> For still 'tis beating in my mind, your reason
> For raising this sea-storm? (I, ii, 175-77)

> A turn or two I'll walk,
> To still my beating mind. (IV, i, 162-63)

> Do not infest your mind with beating on
> The strangeness of this business.
> (V, i, 246-47)

Though Alonso's reflections on his tragic loss are modified by images of the sea and music, he is driven to a sharp outburst by Gonzalo's well-intentioned but irritating attempts to divert him. The feeling of irritation is dramatized by the series of responses in which Alonso tries to keep his temper and silence Gonzalo ("Prithee, peace . . . I prithee, spare . . . prithee, peace . . . prithee, no more").

On the physical level this is similar to the regular pinching and poking that Caliban must endure:

Thou shalt be pinch'd
As thick as honeycomb, each pinch more stinging
Than bees that made 'em.   (I, ii, 328-30)

And at the end of IV, i and in V, i, Caliban, Stephano, Trinculo, Alonso, Antonio, and the rest are tormented and made frantic by this characteristic irritating, persistent punishment.

It is significant, then, that the only flaws which appear in Prospero's character are signs of irritation and impatience, whose motivation is not always fully explained. He is peeved at Miranda in I, ii, and commands her several times to pay better attention, though she is evidently absorbed in his narration. He is harsh with Ariel and Ferdinand, and his disturbance in IV, i goes beyond any reason the plot or his dialogue provide. His irritation is of course consistent with his situation and habits of mind, but its contribution to our theatrical experience is first of all to heighten our awareness of a nagging pulse appearing now here and now there in counterpoint to the strangeness and wonder of the island. The contrast is similar to that between the play's strange, soothing music and its confused noises (from the shouts when the ship splits to the chorus of animal noises which accompanies Ariel's enchanting songs in I, ii, to the noise—it, too, is "strange"—with which the nymphs and reapers vanish in IV, i). The overall effect is at least twofold: the dream-like atmosphere is preserved and heightened, while at the same time we are aware of unpleasant possibilities as of something that at intervals keeps pulsing in the mind.

When the most important instance of disturbance occurs, in IV, i, it makes us fully conscious of the human limitation that the earlier nagging instances have kept suggesting. The masque has provided a vision of abundant, flowering nature, not only of the superhuman cycle, but of a supernatural improvement upon it. Iris reminds us of the cycle of the seasons with a composite of scenes from various times of the year:

Ceres, most bounteous lady, thy rich leas
Of wheat, rye, barley, vetches, oats, and pease;
Thy turfy mountains, where live nibbling sheep,
And flat meads thatch'd with stover, them to keep;
Thy banks with pioned and twilled brims,
Which spongy April at thy hest betrims . . . .
(60-65)

But what Ceres brings the lovers is an eternal abundance. She is pleased that Ferdinand and Miranda are unaffected by Venus's machinations. The rape of Proserpine has limited nature's fruitfulness to half the year, but the lovers are to be exempted from the penalty:

Spring come to you at the farthest
In the very end of harvest! (114-15)

Innocence is to be rewarded with a return to a Golden Age of unfallen nature. Ferdinand is speaking literally when he says:

So rare a wond'red father and a wise
Makes this place Paradise. (123-24)

The dance of the reapers and "temperate" nymphs begins and is interrupted:

They join with the Nymphs in a graceful dance; towards the end whereof Prospero starts suddenly, and speaks; after which, to a strange, hollow, and confused noise, they heavily vanish. (138)

We are returned to the play's anti-music, to the confused noises of the earlier scenes.

The moment particularly echoes the end of the previous scene, in which thunder and lightning have intruded upon the banquet. We have come to associate the noise with the passions of the "men of sin" (perhaps with tragic passion in general) and the discipline to which Prospero is submitting them; and at this point Prospero himself seems to suffer some inner disturbance he has difficulty controlling. His mind is "beating," and Ferdinand and Miranda are upset to see him so agitated. In the speech which follows, Prospero appears to respond to several stimuli: his own disturbance; his children's concern over his passion; and what he seems to regard as Ferdinand's excessive dismay at the dispersal of the masque. Clearly, he feels the Prince has been too deeply engrossed by his entertainment. His argument, however, takes a curious turn. We might expect him to follow this line: Don't worry, this is an illusion, and now I have to turn to something real; life is serious, though under control, and we must put aside vanities. But this is not what he says, and in fact there is little reason to be disturbed by the threat Caliban poses, as the audience knows. In a few lines, Caliban and his friends will be routed by an illusion much cruder than the one we have seen. But the comparison we will make between the vain illusion of the masque and the illusion that tricks Stephano and Trinculo (the work, like the earlier illusory banquet, of the same acting company—Ariel's "rabble") is important, and explains the transition Prospero makes. What you have seen, he says, is mere illusion, and real life . . . that is illusion too, a dream. Here is the crux, the climax of all the strangeness Prospero has provided for us: an illusion which is like life because it reminds us that life is an illusion. We are close to the meaning of the play's carefully established atmosphere—a dream-like reality which readies us not only for the proposition that life is a dream, but that dream, like art, has a vital place in the visionary fabrication we call real life.

The notion of the charm and power of dreams is of course important in the play. There are many references to dreams, and the actors are given a number of opportunities to involve us in their apprehension of the sensation of dreaming. Ferdinand compares the wonder that he feels, the power that subdues his sorrows, to a dream. The Boatswain believes himself to be dreaming. Next to Prospero's, though, the most memorable evocation of the mood of dream—and the one most like Prospero's in its imagery—is Caliban's:

> Be not afeard. The isle is full of noises,
> Sounds and sweet airs, that give delight and hurt not.
> Sometimes a thousand twangling instruments
> Will hum about mine ears, and sometime voices
> That, if I then had wak'd after long sleep,
> Will make me sleep again; and then, in dreaming,
> The clouds methought would open and show riches
> Ready to drop upon me, that, when I wak'd,
> I cried to dream again. (III, ii, 144-52)

The Tempest is, in part, about freedom and limitation and about the paradoxes our desire for freedom involves. Not only Ariel, but Prospero, Ferdinand, and Caliban labor in different ways to be free. Caliban, who is the most intensely limited of the characters, the one most trapped in materiality, has, it is true, the crudest conception of freedom, but he is also allowed to express the most pathetic vision of it. His speech is a tremendously touching account of the effects of Prospero's powers of harmony and illusion on his savage mind, and his description turns on the idea of sleep and dreaming. The beast—or the man—trapped in limitation hears the music of illusion and longs for the illusion to return, as perhaps Ferdinand does when the masque is abruptly cut short. The dream is a source of relief and release, an enchantment that makes life bearable and reveals its wonders. Prospero is the master of illusion, and illusion—like freedom—is something for which our native limitations make us cry out.

Prospero himself recognizes a necessary limit to his art in the unredeemability of Caliban. He is one

on whose nature
Nurture can never stick; on whom my pains,
Humanely taken, all, all lost, quite lost.[3]
(IV, i, 188-90)

But it is also Prospero's awareness of his own sharp passion and his own limitations that prompts him to pardon and set free all his prisoners in a gesture of fundamental kindness:

Hast thou, which art but air, a touch, a feeling
Of their afflictions, and shall not myself,
One of their kind, that relish all as sharply
Passion as they, be kindlier mov'd than thou art?
(V, i, 21-24)

He drowns his book—as earlier Alonso had threatened to drown himself[4]—in order to seek his kind. As he arrives at his final freedom, he abandons his art, his daughter, his servant Ariel, and begins to think of the limits of his own life. ("Every third thought shall be my grave.") Indeed the abandonment of art becomes a frequently repeated, highly visible dramatic motif as the play moves to its close. In the concluding scenes, from the interrupted banquet and the dispersal of the wedding masque, through Prospero's farewell to magic, to the final scene and epilogue, our sense of freedom and limitation is bound up with a strongly evoked sense of what it is like to watch theatrical illusions come to their end. If the atmosphere of wonder and dream is important to *The Tempest*, so is its solemn protracted emphasis on Prospero's abandonment of his powers of enchantment. Even the gesture with which he con-

[3] Prospero's habit of repetition when agitated is another means by which the audience is kept aware of a recurrent pulse of irritability.
[4]   Therefore my son i' th' ooze is bedded, and
I'll seek him deeper than e'er plummet sounded
And with him there lie mudded.
(III, iii, 100-102)

cludes the play reminds us of the power and limits of art, and of its relation to our own limitations and our desire for freedom. It is a moment whose significance will be missed if we fail to visualize the final movement of the characters over the stage:

PROSPERO

Sir, I invite your Highness and your train
To my poor cell...
                    Please you, draw near.
                    Exeunt omnes.
                        (V, i, 300-318)

If *The Tempest* were to end with a procession to some offstage destination (in the manner of, say, *Measure for Measure* or *Cymbeline*), Prospero might be expected to lead the others off—perhaps deferring to Alonso. But here the destination is Prospero's cell, and this has already been localized for us by the "discovery" of Ferdinand and Miranda at line 171. Thus the company would exit by way of this inner stage or "discovery-space," and their exit would constitute an entrance into the cell. The point is that Prospero welcomes them in, they go through the door or curtain, disappear—and Prospero is left alone on the stage to speak the epilogue.

We remember how Prospero has seemed to stage much of the play. In a sense he has staged it all, but more than that, we have seen him staging the masque of the seasons, the banquet in the forest (where his control has been dramatized by the unusual expedient of having him appear "on the top"), the revelation of Ferdinand and Miranda playing chess, and also presiding over the other Ferdinand–Miranda scenes. Indeed, his first entrance provides an opportunity to emphasize the degree to which he has "staged" the storm scene. And now he seems to stage the final disappearance of the characters.

We are thus made specially conscious of his control over the action exactly at the moment—a familiar and

poignant one for playgoers, whatever the play—when
we become aware that it has ended. The effect is to
sharpen the familiar end-of-play emotion, to render it
self-conscious to some degree. Prospero has given the
characters their freedom, and now they have disappeared from our view for good. He has freed us too;
the illusion is over, and we are made strongly aware of
it now as Prospero turns to us. He reminds us that he
is no longer an enchanter, but simply a man. Of course
he is not simply a man, just yet; the play is not entirely
over. He is still an actor in the costume of Prospero
commanding us with all the authority of his art; but
we are watching him begin to shed the wondrous self
he has assumed for the duration of the performance.
He is returning to the role of the ordinary man, and returning us to our ordinary roles as well. For audience
and actor by their mutual presence in the theater have
each been responsible for a wondrous temporary transformation of the other. Prospero is reminding us, too,
that the special glory of his profession, the power to
enchant us in the theater, is a power that lies ultimately in our gift and that it depends on our bodily
participation:

> Now my charms are all o'erthrown,
> And what strength I have's mine own,
> Which is most faint. . . .
>   Now I want
> Spirits to enforce, art to enchant,
> And my ending is despair,
> Unless I be reliev'd by prayer,
> Which pierces so that it assaults
> Mercy itself and frees all faults.
> As you from crimes would pardon'd be,
> Let your indulgence set me free. (1-20)

He is strictly governed by human limitation; he has
only his own strength to rely on. He asks us to set him
free, again by a gesture of human kindness. He asks

that our applause rise to heaven, and his language once more reminds us of wondrous dream-like apparitions in the sky, such as Caliban saw ("The clouds methought would open and show riches") or of the cloud-capped towers that, like the Globe itself, fade into thin air.

There is a peculiar doubleness to our sense of life in the moments after a play has ended. We find ourselves unusually sensitive to ordinary reality, because we have been returned to it with a shock. At the same time, we are still subject to the illusion we have witnessed; it persists in the world around us, in the shape of the dialogue we overhear, and very likely in our walk, speech, and body image. Shakespeare has played upon this aftereffect before, notably in *Twelfth Night*, but never has it been so richly bound up with the experience of an entire play.

We are left with an impression, then, that fuses a sense of the nature and power of drama with the power of kindness in life. The transition from play to epilogue in *The Tempest* makes us strongly conscious once more of Prospero's powers, his abandonment of them, and of their relation to our own experience. The play is over; it has passed like a dream. It has had something of the natural strangeness of a dream, too, if staged correctly, but we also remember as Prospero leaves us, as our "freedom" is restored, that life is like a dream, leaving not a wrack behind. The experience we have just had has been illusion; it has been the product of art. And art, as Prospero's magic has made clear, is finally most like life in that it has its limits—a fact that Shakespeare has exploited throughout his career. The end of illusion heightens our sense of illusion and of its interpenetration with "reality." When the characters are finally freed, they cease to exist and return us to the limits of our own condition—which gestures of deeply shared humanity may momentarily redeem. We too depend on kindness and our capacity to imagine it. Like Caliban and Prospero, we must seek for grace.

The very evanescence of all that we desire most radically from life—the fragility of those instants in which we seem at one with the cycle of natural restoration—has been the source and subject of this final moment of drama. Life is a dream, and dream is a deeply needed mode of apprehending reality. Indeed all effort to grasp reality is a kind of dream. Drama is of all art forms the most ostentatiously impermanent because it makes the most immediate connection with our bodies. If it has a special power to open us to life, to release as in our deepest self the illuminating energies of the superhuman cycle, the lucidity of such moments, to be true, cannot be permanent. The satisfyingly clear vision is designed to fade. The theater is like a dream. But it is most like a dream in its strange specificity, its peculiar fusion of intimacy and remoteness, of irreality and inescapable bodily presence. If the theater is a place of illusion, it is also a place where illusions are stripped away. The theater, like Prospero's island—and like festivity, mercy, love, or even the notion of freedom—is at once an escape from the self and a confrontation of it. Enchantment and disenchantment are a twin birth of our awareness of limitation. We discover the most truth about ourselves by attempting to grasp the phantoms we create, which fade into thin air. *Alles Vergängliche ist nur ein Gleichnis.*

Appendices

"Self" in Shakespeare and the *OED*

The *OED* is misleading about Shakespeare's use of "self," but for what I think are understandable reasons and in a way that points to the interesting pressures the word is under in Shakespeare's work. The editors very naturally divide the word into its pronominal and substantive uses, and distinguish as the first type of the substantive, "the pronominal notion expressed substantively." This is a simple enough category, applying to contexts like "Me and thy crying self." Here the word is still simply a grammatical indicator. Seven substantive definitions of "self" follow, of which four (nos. 2, 5, 6, and 7) have no bearing on this discussion. The other three are given as follows:

3. That which in a person is really and intrinsically *he* (in contradistinction to what is adventitious); the ego (often identified with the soul or mind as opposed to the body); a permanent subject of successive and varying states of consciousness.

4*a*. What one is at a particular time or in a particular aspect or relation; one's nature, character, or (sometimes) physical constitution or appearance, considered as different at different times. Chiefly with qualifying adj., (*one's*) *old, former, later self*.

4*b*. An assemblage of characteristics and dispositions which may be conceived as constituting one of various conflicting personalities within a human being.

The earliest example of 3 cited is from Traherne in 1674. We may allow that there is no clear-cut Shakespearean example of 3, precisely construed—though a case could be made for:

> Property was thus appalled,
> That the self was not the same.

For 4*b* the earliest example is from Spenser's *Amoretti*, 1595:

> And in my selfe, my inward selfe I meane,
> Most liuely lyke behold your semblant trew.
> (XLV, 3-4)

It is a questionable choice since by "inward selfe" Spenser clearly intends nothing more than (as he goes on to say) "my hart."[1] This is a true substantive use, but it does not support the definition given.

The first example given of 4*a* is from Dryden in 1697. But surely this is exactly the sense of "self" involved when the newly crowned Henry V says:

> Presume not that I am the thing I was;
> For God doth know, so shall the world perceive,
> That I have turn'd away my former self.
> (2 *Henry IV*, v, v, 60-62)

Now this is one of at least six instances of "self" in Shakespeare which raise further questions. I number them for convenience in the discussion which follows:

1. That I have turn'd away my former self.
2. Let me lodge Lichas on the horns o' th' moon;
   And with those hands, that grasp'd the heaviest club,
   Subdue my worthiest self.
   (*Antony and Cleopatra*, IV, xii, 45-47)
3. I have a kind of self resides with you;
   But an unkind self, that itself will leave
   To be another's fool.
   (*Troilus and Cressida*, III, ii, 155-57)
4. Property was thus appalled,
   That the self was not the same.
   (*The Phoenix and Turtle*, 37-38)

---

[1] *The Works of Edmund Spenser: The Minor Poems*, ed. Charles Osgood and Henry Lotspeich, II (Baltimore, 1947), 214.

5. Let my unsounded self, suppos'd a fool,
   Now set thy long-experienc'd wit to school.
                                    (*Lucrece*, 1819-20)
6. For, having traffic with thyself alone,
   Thou of thyself thy sweet self dost deceive.
                                    (Sonnets, 4, 9-10)

About each of these, one of three assumptions must be true:

A. It has been overlooked by the editors.
B. The editors consider it an example of definition 4*b*.
C. It is considered pronominal by the editors.

A certainly cannot be true of all six. *B* may just possibly apply to 2 and 6. 5 was published before the Spenser example. No one, I take it, would claim that *B* applies to the others. That leaves us with *C* as the probable explanation of most if not all the examples. Plainly, 5 and 6 may both be read as pronominal. But here we strike upon the crucial point. By insisting on a sharp distinction between pronominal and substantive uses, we find ourselves unable to accommodate occasions when the difference is split, or when, in the act of expressing the pronominal notion substantively, "self" acquires richer associations. When Shakespeare writes

   For, having traffic with thyself alone,
   Thou of thyself thy sweet self dost deceive

it would be inaccurate to say that he is deliberately and simply distinguishing a component of the personality and calling it the sweet self. If Shakespeare were somehow compelled to paraphrase these lines, he might well say they warn the young man not to cheat himself of himself and only add by way of epithet the notion that he is a sweet person. Yet this would not do justice to the poem. It is true the sonnets never explicitly state that the young man is anything but sweet—but of course they imply the opposite regularly. And the line itself forces us by its rhythm, syntax, and sense to give more substance and analytic distinction to "self" than its ostensible pronominal function requires.

A stronger case than this could be made for the non-pronominal meaning of "self" here and in *Lucrece*, 1819. But the minimum argument is sufficient for my purposes and, I think, more closely reflects the movements of meaning in the poem (the activity of Shakespeare's mind, if you will) in dealing with what we would call today ideas about the self. A similar movement or pressure may be felt in a number of instances of "self" I have not listed. For instance, in *The Comedy of Errors*, the insistence on Antipholus's search for identity[2] joins with recurrent references to self to give the following passages an added resonance, though "self" and "thyself" are primarily pronominal:

> How comes it now, my husband, O, how comes it,
> That thou art then estranged from thyself?
> Thyself I call it, being strange to me,
> That, undividable, incorporate,
> Am better than thy dear self's better part.
> Ah, do not tear away thyself from me!
>
> (II, ii, 121-26)

[2] See above, p. 18. In an early soliloquy Antipholus expresses his problem as a loss of self, a search for self:

> ANTIPHOLUS
> Farewell till then. I will go lose myself,
> And wander up and down to view the city.
> MERCHANT
> Sir, I commend you to your own content.
> *Exit.*
> ANTIPHOLUS
> He that commends me to mine own content
> Commends me to the thing I cannot get.
> I to the world am like a drop of water
> That in the ocean seeks another drop,
> Who, falling there to find his fellow forth,
> Unseen, inquisitive, confounds himself.
> So I, to find a mother and a brother,
> In quest of them, unhappy, lose myself.
>
> (I, ii, 30-40)

It is thyself, mine own self's better part,
Mine eye's clear eye, my dear heart's dearer heart.
(III, ii, 61-62)

The resonance is at least as strong in Gonzalo's speech
from the last act of *The Tempest*:

O, rejoice
Beyond a common joy, and set it down
With gold on lasting pillars: in one voyage
Did Claribel her husband find at Tunis,
And Ferdinand, her brother, found a wife
Where he himself was lost, Prospero his dukedom
In a poor isle, and all of us ourselves
When no man was his own. (v, i, 206-13)

And in *Hamlet*, the concerns of the play and the rhythm
of the line are working to deepen the substantive
suggestions of "self" in "This above all: to thine own
self be true." It might be added, too, that once the effect
of "self" in Sonnet 4 has been felt and the arguments
of the sequence begin to sink in, the references to self
in 1, 126, and 151—on first reading simply pronominal
—become more complex.

We are left, however, with examples 1-4 and the apparently paradoxical conclusion that C is the most
likely explanation for them. It is of course possible that
the compilers of the *OED* overlooked four or more oc-
currences in Shakespeare of a familiar and important
word used in a common modern sense otherwise un-
recorded before the Restoration. But it seems more reasonable to conclude that they must have considered at
least some of these instances esssentially pronominal,
and the best explanation I can find for this is that the
editors responsible for the entry had fallen into the
habit of seeing all kinds of slippery Shakespearean examples as merely pronominal by virtue of having to
insist on a hard and fast distinction between pronomi-

nal and substantive in the many borderline cases that Shakespeare presents.[3]

[3] They would certainly not have been alone in considering "self" exclusively pronominal. The authoritative Shakespearean dictionary of the day, Schmidt's *Shakespeare-Lexicon* (3d ed., rev., Berlin and New York, 1902), gives only one substantive meaning for "self": "one's own person, the identical individual."

Examples of Movement and Spectacle in Three Early Plays

In Chapter VIII I refer to Shakespeare's handling of stage movement on a large scale in three very early plays. These are further notes on the subject.

Titus Andronicus, First Scene

At the start we are made aware of three foci of attention on the stage. On one side Saturninus, on the other Bassianus, each with his followers poised in opposition, on the verge of combat. Above center, the Tribunes and Senate, attempting to mediate between them; they only succeed when at line 17 Marcus enters carrying the crown. With the crown present aloft, the tension eases, the soldiers are dismissed, Bassianus and Saturninus mount the upper stage, awaiting Titus. He enters as part of a grand processional requiring the full resources of the company—"as many as can be." There is a curious, even disturbing cast to this triumphal march, as the very full stage directions make clear:

Sound drums and trumpets, and then enter two of Titus's sons; and then two Men *bearing a coffin covered with black; then two other sons.* Then TITUS ANDRONICUS; *and then* TAMORA, *the Queen of Goths and her sons* DEMETRIUS, *and* CHIRON; *and with* AARON *the Moor, and others as many as can be. Then set down the coffin, and Titus speaks.* (69)

The coffin is the surprise—the suggestion of an obscure and unpleasant ritual at the heart of this great assertion of order—and the staging emphasizes its presence. It is brought on early and set down after all the marchers have entered and taken their places on stage;

our eyes are drawn to it. This entrance calls attention to a fourth focal area—the tomb of the Andronici. The crown is above, the tomb below; the victory march honors a black coffin (and includes the menacing figures of Aaron the Moor and the dusky Tamora). Titus's opening words seem to articulate the peculiar charged quality of this atmosphere:

Hail, Rome, victorious in thy mourning weeds!

The magniloquent association of triumph with death, of the crown with the tomb, strikes a resonant note for the play that follows.

The tomb is opened and remains gaping while Alarbus is sacrificed offstage and Tamora, onstage, pleads for her son's life. It continues to be important, both literally and as a symbol, throughout the scene as Titus, who has buried sons in glory at the beginning, now angrily kills another son and is at length persuaded to grant him burial too. Before Mutius is interred, however, the tensely held order of the forces massed onstage shatters and the outbursts of anger and physical violence lead to a shift in power, signalized by the appearance of Tamora, Aaron, and her two sons aloft (298) with the new Emperor, who denounces Titus. Titus's new position is reflected in the scene's second burial. The ceremony at the tomb is no longer public and glorious but private and pathetic. The crowds have gone and Titus is alone with his family, distressed by them, spurned by Saturninus.

We are left with a sense not only of personal violence, but of some radical upheaval in the state—in the life of all the bodies on the stage. Moreover the scene has established certain dramatic symbols clearly and emphatically, with perfect ease in the midst of vast turbulence and excitement. The strained but apparently necessary relation between crown and tomb both prepares for and deepens the drama of mutilation and lament to come.

Henry VI, Part One

Think of the bodies of Shakespeare's company en masse, especially as it must have been early in his career—young, athletic, trained in acrobatic display and imitations of combat, a troupe of tumblers and fencers as well as mimes and orators. And then think of how the sweep of athletic bodies across the stage is used in *1 Henry VI* not only to provide an exciting spectacle but to focus and clarify, to render dramatic, the entire unwieldy chronicle. The military events abound in opportunities for athleticism and spectacle. Walls are scaled or leapt over, people appear "on the top" or "on the turret"; a man is shot in what must be a "special effect." A very simple pattern emerges from the battles, however, which the spectacle urges upon us. What Talbot keeps winning by courage and immense physical exertion is lost by cunning—first through deceit and witchcraft on the field and in the end through dissension at home. And the inglorious, unmilitary but often large-scale combats in the English scenes help make the point. Battle and witchcraft in France; squabble and politics at home.

Talbot is defeated only because of weakness and double-dealing among the English nobility. His death marks the intersection of the political and military plots of the play, which has begun appropriately enough with a funeral. This is the first of a number of scenes in which noble bodies are carried off the stage with special comment and conveyance, and here too a dramatic pattern is established through spectacle. There are five such scenes, some less ceremonious than others, but all accompanied by energetic praise of the dead:

Henry V (I, i; general eulogies)
Salisbury and Gargrave (I, iv; Talbot eulogizes)
Mortimer (II, v; York eulogizes)

Bedford (III, ii; Talbot eulogizes)
Talbot and his son (IV, vii; Lucy eulogizes)

The valedictory mood, the sense of a great past gone
is, of course, important. More to the point, each of
these distinguished Englishmen has been in some sense
betrayed.

Henry VI, Part Two

The other ceremonial scenes in *I Henry VI* regularly
give way to squabbling and even to pitched battle. The
meaning of this is plain enough, but it is only in Part
Two that the device is used with any real sophistication. Instead of repeated outbursts of roughly the same
intensity, the disruptions that run through the play
form a larger pattern of their own—but one example of
the greater interest in shaping that Part Two exhibits.

The pattern, simply described, is one of increasing
violence, more and more out of control and increasingly massive and savage. This follows the pattern of
the plot, in which increasingly serious threats to the
crown emerge, from Eleanor to York. In the first two
acts the moments of violence are all relatively contained and are fully controlled by authority—the arrest
of Eleanor (I, iv), whipping of Simpcox (II, i), victory
of Peter over Horner (II, iii). In Act III, "two or three"
murderers run over the stage between scenes i and ii,
having killed Gloucester, but they are furtive, quiet.
Gloucester's death is announced in III, ii, a scene interrupted by repeated crowd noises offstage and sudden
intrusions upon the King's presence (Warwick and Suffolk enter at one point with drawn swords). The increase in uncontrolled violence is neatly marked by the
transition from III, ii to IV, i. The farewells of Margaret
and Suffolk ("This way fall I to death. . . This way for
me"—a symmetrical exeunt followed by the discovery
of the Cardinal in bed, probably in the curtained area
center stage, the spatial arrangement linking the two

events) are followed by the Cardinal's hysterical death in III, iii. Henry concludes the scene with the solemn, "And let us all to meditation." The stage direction that immediately follows his exit provides maximum contrast:

Alarum. Fight at sea. Ordnance goes off.

Next, of course, there is Cade's conspiracy, and the stage is full of greater turmoil and battle. A new note of open savagery is introduced: beginning with Act IV, heads appear on stage—Suffolk's (twice), Say's, Cromer's, and Cade's. Finally in Act V York succeeds Cade as the primary threat to the crown, and the entire company is divided into two warring factions—visibly. In V, i these huge teams are massed on stage before the battle of St. Albans. Everything in the theater now is bent on war, and we are ready for the horror and cruelty of the rest of the tetralogy.

APPENDIX C

Comic Expectation in
Measure for Measure

I have pointed out that in *Hamlet* and *King Lear* audience expectation is sometimes turned against itself to produce a comment on the action. We experience not only suspense or surprise but a heightened awareness of the dramatic appetite aroused and an attachment of that appetite, in what might be called a subverted form, to the play's themes. It seems to me that the "problem" comedies might profitably be studied with this technique in mind; what follows is no more than a sketch for such an analysis of *Measure for Measure*.

Measure for Measure is often discussed as a kind of potential or partial tragedy out of which comedy has been made. The trouble with this approach lies in the implication that the tragedy is somehow prior to the comedy. This is very misleading, particularly with regard to the final scene. For though we are meant to feel genuinely dangerous energies in the play's middle passages, our expectation is comic from the start.[1] The exposition (I, i-iii, especially the scene with Friar Thomas) encourages definite assumptions. We guess that with the Duke away serious flaws will begin to appear in the administration of justice in Vienna. But we also expect that the real malefactors will eventually be discovered, Angelo's true character will reveal itself, and the Duke will step forward at the right moment— when the situation is at its clearest and most hopeless —to punish or improve the sinners and to set everything

[1] One might compare Marston's *Malcontent*, in which the resolution is comic but the initial expectation is not.

to rights in an exemplary way, probably better than before. And of course all this happens. The problem, then, is not that the play's finale is a surprise or violates our original expectations. Even as we watch Angelo, Isabella, and Claudio suffer their irretrievable scenes, we know that the entertainment we are watching proposes to retrieve them. We expect something like the final scene just as we expect Hamlet to kill Claudius or Achilles to kill Hector. But the journey to that conclusion is full of surprises and complications, and these color our reaction at the end. Some sense of complication is with us from the opening lines. We are quickly aware that an obscure intention is unfolding, and that it will involve the exposure of at least one character, Angelo, to an unsettling test. At the end of the first scene our attention is made to rest on Angelo and on the strangeness of his sudden accession to power. The cue for it is a passage that may seem insignificant on the page:

ANGELO
. . . Let us withdraw together,
And we may soon our satisfaction have
Touching that point.
ESCALUS
I'll wait upon your honour. *Exeunt.*

"I'll wait upon your honour," is a typical exit line but here it reflects the new relation between Escalus and Angelo. Escalus is "first in question," clearly the man one would expect the Duke to have made his deputy. Both Angelo and Escalus are puzzled, perhaps bewildered by the Duke's decision. Angelo has protested his appointment. He seems confused as to what has happened and unready for his new authority. His "Let us withdraw together" may suggest deference to Escalus; it tends at least to put him on a footing of equality, while Escalus's answer insists, quite properly, on

Angelo's preeminence. The actor playing Angelo must respond to this and lead the way offstage. Thus both actors are given a chance to register awkwardness in adjusting to their new positions, an early indication that government—personal and public—is coming under stress.

"Your scope is as mine own," the Duke has told Angelo, and "scope" is an important word in the play, particularly when coupled with "restraint":

As surfeit is the father of much fast,
So every scope by the immoderate use
Turns to restraint.   (I, ii, 130-32)

Ay, just; perpetual durance, a restraint,
Though all the world's vastidity you had,
To a determin'd scope.   (III, i, 68-70)

Both words reflect the elusive problems of definition and limit raised by the idea of justice in *Measure for Measure*. "Scope" suggests not only liberty but license— an opportunity for "too much liberty" (I, ii, 129)—but it also suggests limitation, a prescribed arena in which one is free to move. "Restraint" implies a loss of liberty, but (to a lesser degree) suggests control and balance as well. Scope is the more important word, and its ambiguity brings us close to the central processes of the play. Its meaning changes easily into its opposite— liberty passing into limit, something expansive passing into something painful as sexual satisfaction passes into disease. In this it is like our everyday sense of justice, since "justice'" implies a joyous healthy order but can in practice be painful or repressive. The power of "scope" and "restraint" and their cognate expressions in *Measure for Measure* is that they do not simply suggest justice and mercy, but that both suggest both, as well as the opposites of both. And in this they reflect a problematic aspect of justice and mercy that the play repeatedly exhibits. Though justice and mercy have their separate and theologically well-defined claims, human justice is often actually unjust when it leaves mercy out of account, just as mercy by itself can often prove a bawd, a mask for permissiveness. Because man is weak and ignorant, because he is most ignorant of what he's most assured, his justice and mercy are constantly passing into their opposites.

Midway through the final scene, Angelo angrily responds to Mariana's accusations:

> I did but smile till now.
> Now, good my lord, give me the scope of justice.
> (233-34)

The double edge of both "scope" and "justice" is felt in the irony of his request. We know that Angelo will receive "the scope of justice" in a way he does not expect; he will be humiliated and condemned. What we may not guess is that he will be pardoned, a third meaning for the phrase.

The play moves from the scope of the stews to the restraint of the prison (which, as Pompey tells us, comes to house much of the stews' population). At the same time the play tests Angleo and Isabella, both of whom prefer restraint, by giving them scope. In their holding back from sexual engagement and responsibility in the great world, Angelo and Isabella are examples of the unsounded self. Directly or through the plot he sets in motion, the Duke forces upon them opportunities for public and private action that release surprising energies within them, that cause them to break down and lash out—as when Isabella denounces her brother; and when the strain of their new scope is at the height he tests them again, by applying restraint. As he has tested Angelo by giving him the scope of office, he now tests him by discovery and the threat of death, and he tests Isabella by giving her sway over Angelo's life. By the time the Duke has carried the plot through to its conclusion, Angelo, Isabella, and Claudio have each experienced "the scope of justice" in all the competing senses of the phrase.

The problem of government is to arrive at a just balance of scope and restraint. Every scope by the immoderate use turns to restraint, and we have powerful examples in the play of immoderate restraint leading to an unpleasant or cruel exercise of scope. At the center of the play, very close together, come three outbursts—Angelo's, Isabella's, and Claudio's (frightened of death, he urges his sister to comply with Angelo's request)[2]—three disturbing soundings of the self produced by the Duke's experiment. As the Duke has tested the characters, so now their reactions test the comic promise he has made us. The outbursts prepare us for the turn of the play, in which the Duke—speaking in prose and introducing us to great blocks of exposition and planned intrigue—must take busy charge of events in order to pursue the comic resolution. From the point of view of our expectations the play at this point poses a group of questions that involve scope and restraint. How can Angelo, Isabella, and Claudio be freed from the dangerous situation, physical and spiritual, that the plot and their outbursts have trapped them in? How can our view of their world be changed from tears to laughter? How can the feeling of an unfolding, which we have been led to expect and demand, be adjusted—without artistic inepititude—to the situation's emotional and moral intricacies?

The play turns, as everyone agrees, at III, i, 152, but the change of direction does not come as a surprise. We have been waiting all along for the Duke to take charge, though we may have been troubled by the intensity of the complications. What *is* surprising is the turn that comes in IV, ii. Here our expectations are genuinely

---

[2] I don't mean to suggest we find Claudio's reaction as unsympathetic as Angelo's or even Isabella's. But it is an outburst, it breaks through the self-possessed image Claudio has tried to maintain, and it is disturbing.

upset because the Duke himself is upset. Once again a close look at the text shows how our attention is focused and our expectations carefully raised.

The Duke arrives, inquiring whether any message has come. It takes some time for the messenger to be admitted and the dialogue calls attention to the fact:

DUKE
How now! what noise?[3] That spirit's possess'd with haste
That wounds the unsisting postern with these strokes.
PROVOST
There he must stay until the officer
Arise to let him in.   (IV, ii, 91-94)

The buildup continues. The Duke is eager, expectant, the Provost dubious:

DUKE
Have you no countermand for Claudio yet
But he must die to-morrow
PROVOST
            None, sir, none.
DUKE
As near the dawning, Provost, as it is,
You shall hear more ere morning.
PROVOST
            Happily
You something know, yet I believe there comes
No countermand.   (95-100)

Finally the messenger enters and our expectation is heightened further because the appearance of Angelo's man seems suddenly to convince the Provost that the Duke is right:

[3] The Duke has already referred to the knocking three lines earlier ("Now are they come,"), so this is to alert the Provost to the sound and the audience to the Duke's impatience. (With the Folio I keep the Provost onstage here. Cf. J. W. Lever's Arden edition.)

DUKE
This is his lordship's man.
PROVOST
And here comes Claudio's pardon.[4]
(103-104)

The Duke summarizes exultantly:

This is his pardon, purchas'd by such sin
For which the pardoner himself is in.
Hence hath offence his quick celerity,
When it is borne in high authority.
When vice makes mercy, mercy's so extended,
That for the fault's love is the offender friended.
(111-16)

And only then does the revelation come:

"Whatsoever you may hear to the contrary, let
Claudio be executed by four of the clock; and in the
afternoon Barnardine. . . ." What say you to this, sir?
(123-31)

The Duke does not respond directly. His reply shows
that he has been thinking furiously:

What is that Barnardine who is to be executed in
the afternoon? (132-33)

The expected development of the action has been un-
derlined, our emotional investment in it has been increased, and then the worst has happened. We still
expect the comic resolution—the play admits of no
other—but the Duke will have to scramble for it.

His efforts accompany our own mental efforts to grasp
the turn the plot has taken. Angelo has refused, as it
were, to be vanquished by the simple assertion of comic
providence; he persists in the character the play has
discovered for him. In watching the Duke scramble to
get the better of the situation, we experience the effort

[4] I follow the Folio assignment of speeches.

170

of the comic plot to master its difficult materials, which is at the same time the effort of an entirely benign justice (for that is what the Duke and comedy in their joint mastery have promised us) to enact itself in the stews and prisons and among the Angelos and Isabellas, the Froths and Elbows of Vienna. It does not take the Duke long to recover, but until the matter of Barnardine is settled and the convenient solution of Ragozine proposed, we are likely to be impressed by the fact that Pompey—who now interrupts the action with his monologue, "I am as well acquainted here as I was in our house of profession"—is more confidently at home in the place of restraint than the busily improvising Duke. Once Ragozine is thought of, the Duke's control is reestablished, but our response to his masterful display of scope and restraint in the finale will be affected by what we have just seen.

At the end justice is remarkably sure, satisfying, lucid. But this has only been made possible by elaborate contrivance, a play-full of preparation, masquerade, and good luck, the happy mechanics of comedy. For four acts, the play has reminded us that justice may ordinarily be scarcely wiser than iniquity. Indeed, when the Duke leaves the stage halfway through the final scene, we are reminded of this once again, since Escalus is not very successful at untangling the puzzle left him. He is, in fact, considerably less effective and humane than he has been with Elbow and Froth (II, i). But with the Duke present, justice is free from its ordinary restraints. All difficulties are but easy when they are known. And since no harm has finally been done, no mortal penalties need be exacted.

Claudio is not dead, but the pretence that he is has its effect on us as well as on Isabella. While we watch the last scene we entertain a thought there is seldom room for in the resolving moments of comedy: "It might easily have been otherwise and much worse." The pattern of justice here, in which every ambiguity is sorted out and every loss restored, in which everyone is punished according to his deserts and every punishment improves, is ideal, but it depends on the special dispensation of theatrical contrivance. We enjoy it, but the play has seen to it that our enjoyment depends on our recognition of the distance it maintains from the restraints and dangerous scope of real life.

Just as the journey we have taken to reach the finale colors our response to it, so our comic expectations will have modified our responses along the way. The central scenes, with all their terrible human complexity, must strike us as somehow reconcilable, in dramatic terms, to the Duke's comic power over the action and his promise to test the characters on behalf of justice. We know that something will intervene to rescue the action from its consequences. We know that Claudio and Isabella will be spared, and perhaps Angelo too. What happens is that we are forced to wonder just how their situation can be retrieved in an artistically satisfying way, how justice, that is, can be done on this stage. Our dramatic appetite thus becomes attached to our understanding of justice. This makes us all the more aware, as the final scene unfolds, that it is only by virtue of the comic convention that justice is actually accomplished. The play has promised from the start to unfold the properties of government, and the Angelo–Isabella scenes remind us that government finally must come up against the individual self, in all its baffling duplicity and fear. Only a divine authority, or one granted the absolute and benign power over action that comedy grants the Duke, can govern such subjects with perfect justice.

If the experience of the play does not support an attitude that is "optimistic" in terms a secular and problem-solving society can easily accept, neither is it cynical or pessimistic. There is a pleasure in the resolution that depends on all that has gone before. As the end approaches and Angelo's trial begins, what we want is justice, justice, justice, justice! We get it to perfection, as emblematic and unambiguous a revelation as at the end of *Hamlet*—after a nearly comparable tangle of seeming and doubt. The comic release is the equivalent of the exercise of a justice such as we never cease to desire in life; it is a justice that discovers the wicked and rewards the good, improves all and harms none—that can be of a piece with mercy and yet not fail in scope or restraint. When we watch Lucio falling into the trap, even setting it for himself, being irrepressibly impertinent in just the way that will embarrass him most and make his wickedness clearest, when we see him after that moving to unmask the Duke, we feel it is wonderful, more than we had expected the comedy could provide, too good to be true. But though there is an irony here, it is not bitter or negative. It is a superbly engineered cue for comic release; we anticipate it with relish and greet it with joy. And our persisting memory of what we have witnessed for nearly four acts—the impossible and painfully familiar tangle of just and unjust in public and private life—this counterpoint to our comic joy has its carefully prepared place in the meaning of the drama. The Duke's severe insistence on testing souls, the Christian pressure he brings to bear on Juliet, Claudio, and Isabella as well as Angelo, point to last things, to the kingdom of heaven. The joy we feel at the play's end is a joy no exercise of government in this world can ever attain. Without comedy, the Vienna we are shown so realistically would remain boiling and bubbling in its corruption. But our pleasure in the play reflects a source of joy that clearly is meant to govern our worldly arrangements as much as possible. As Shakespeare is at pains to remind us in another play written at this time, "All's well that ends well" refers not only to the structure of comedy but to the design of a Christian life. The end of *Measure for Measure* refers us to the kingdom of heaven—and to the earthly reflection of its joys in mercy and marriage and comedy—while allowing us to feel very plainly that its order is not to be achieved on earth.

Index

175